HISTORIC
Houses & Gardens
of WARWICK

To Maureen and Bob

Christine Cluley & Jennifer Meir

Best wishes

Christine

AMBERLEY

The oldest building in Warwick.

First published 2012

Amberley Publishing
The Hill, Stroud
Gloucestershire, GL5 4EP

www.amberleybooks.com

British Library Cataloguing in Publication Data.
A catalogue record for this book is available from the British Library.

ISBN 978 1 4456 0742 9

Typeset in 10pt on 12pt Sabon.
Typesetting and Origination by Amberley Publishing.
Printed in the UK.

Contents

Map of Warwick

The common, the racecourse and the town.

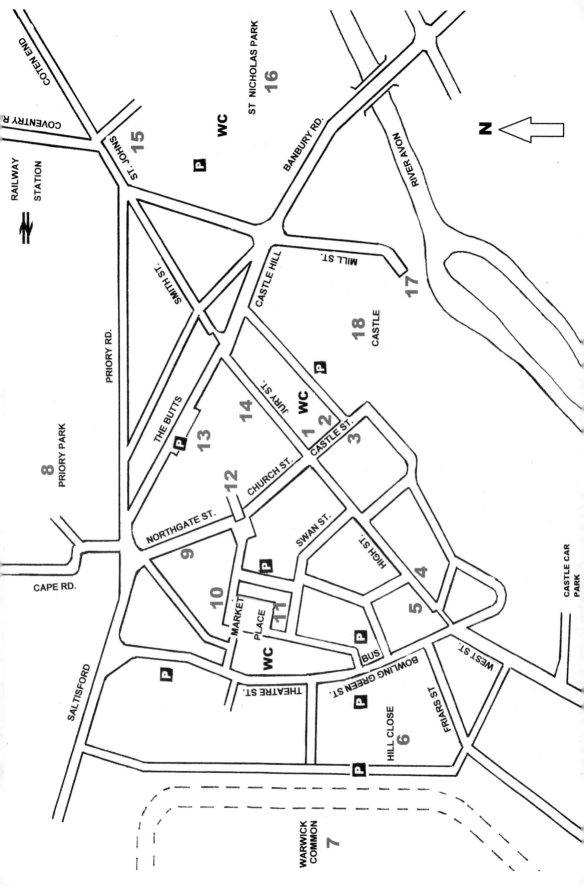

Foreword
Message from the Mayor of Warwick, Councillor Trudy Offer

Just as Christine Cluley has written *Warwick: A Short History and Guide* she now leads us, in partnership with Jennifer Meir, to the following, which gives us a quick reference to Warwick's historic buildings and gardens open for public appreciation. With a deft style delivered from a solid historical knowledge base we are led through and to the many beautiful buildings and gardens which even those of us who are lucky enough to live in Warwick sometimes overlook in our familiarity. Yet when we meet visitors and want to show them around our wonderful town we rediscover how lucky we are. This book is a most excellent companion for all who wish to sample the delights and dip their toes into the pool of historic Warwick.

I am naturally particularly proud of Warwick and the Courthouse in which the Mayor and Town Council and Visitor Information Centre presides. We are delighted and express our thanks to the Heritage Lottery Fund that our bid for the restoration of the Courthouse has been successful. The bid unlocks the future of the building, for Warwick's local community and visitors to the town.

Cllr Trudy Offer

The summerhouse in the Master's Garden.

Introduction

This book provides a description of the historic buildings and gardens open to the public in the town of Warwick. A short history is given for each entry, together with a description of the house or garden as it is today, and details of when the site is open. A map of the town is also provided. The book is not intended to be completely comprehensive but offers an overview of this historic town.

Warwick is an old town whose origins lie in the Saxon period. The town's historic past is reflected in the wealth of old buildings still remaining, of which the castle, Lord Leycester Hospital and St Mary's Collegiate Church are the outstanding examples. The historic town is still contained within walls that were started in the years after the Conquest but were possibly never completed. Warwick was granted charters that allowed it to hold markets and, as the town prospered, to establish a Corporation to manage its affairs.

In 1694 a disastrous fire swept through Warwick. Although the town had some stone buildings, many of the houses were half-timbered and had thatched roofs that caught fire easily and intensified the blaze. The fire also spread rapidly through the back garden areas, where numerous outhouses, piggeries and other buildings were also thatched. The west end of St Mary's Church, in the centre of town, was gutted and was later rebuilt with a fine new tower. The centre of the town now has many houses built in the late seventeenth-century style, such as those in Northgate Street, where most of the old half-timbered houses were rebuilt in stone within three years of the fire. A tradition of skilled craftsmen in the town contributed to the high standard of many of the new houses built in the eighteenth century. Among their number were master masons and builders such as Francis Smith, who built the Court House in 1725–28, and was twice mayor of Warwick, and the Hiorn brothers, who were largely responsible for the rebuilding of the new Shire Hall.

Many of the eighteenth-century changes were introduced by successive Lords Brooke of Warwick Castle. In 1709 Lord Brooke gave money towards the setting up of a racecourse, and the first horse races were held on a course running around the Common. Warwick Races are still popular today. A later Lord Brooke, Francis Greville, created Earl of Warwick in 1759, decided to alter his grounds to the new informal landscape style. He asked Lancelot (Capability) Brown, then at the beginning of his career, to redesign both the gardens and the park. In the 1780s the second Earl of Warwick, George Greville, obtained an Act of Parliament to enable him to build a new bridge spanning the Avon upstream from the castle, since the old medieval bridge was too narrow for the traffic it carried and was badly in need of repair. Mill Street, which originally led into the town from the old bridge, has some picturesque old buildings and now makes a peaceful backwater for residents and visitors alike to enjoy. There is a most attractive modern garden at the bottom of Mill Street, opposite the ruins of the old bridge.

During the eighteenth century some very fine public buildings were constructed and are still in use today. Very little public or private building was carried out during Victorian

St Nicholas Park.

times in Warwick. There was a growth in population and this led to the provision of homes in the suburbs. In 1851 came the arrival of the railway, which made a great difference to the ease of travel for the majority. In 1881 the Leamington & Warwick tramway was started, using horse-drawn vehicles until electricity was installed in 1905. The open spaces such as the Common and St Nicholas Park became increasingly popular, with the park becoming the main centre in the town for public gardens and sports facilities. Warwick, however, lacked industry, and although it was the county town it never became large enough to rival Coventry, nor did it have the attractions of the spa waters, the Pump Rooms and the royal connection of nearby Royal Leamington Spa.

In the middle of the nineteenth century Hill Close Gardens were laid out overlooking the racecourse and the Common. These leisure gardens, created for the townsfolk to use mainly at weekends, have recently been restored. They are of particular interest since such gardens were once to be found on the outskirts of every town, and the majority have been lost due to modern development.

Warwick's old market still provides a bustling presence in the square on Saturdays. Its charter dates from the thirteenth century, and farmers bring in local produce much as they must always have done in past times. Today the town is lively, with new shops and restaurants filling the old buildings, visitors and locals alike enjoying the modern amenities set within historic surroundings.

The Bear and Ragged Staff

The bear and ragged staff were originally the heraldic badges of the earls of Warwick. Their origins lie in the medieval earls' family myths. Sir William Dugdale, writing in the 1650s, said that Arthgal, an earl of Warwick at the time of King Arthur, thought that his name came from the Latin word *ursus*, which means bear. Dugdale also suggested that the ragged staff was chosen because Mordivus, Earl of Warwick, killed a giant with a broken branch of a tree. Of course, neither of these earls ever really existed and Dugdale was just recalling medieval legends handed down through the ages. The bear was quite a common heraldic device and implied boldness and courage. In the Beauchamp Chapel there are several examples of the badge on which the bear and ragged staff are used separately.

The first person known to have them together was Richard Neville, Earl of Warwick, called 'Warwick the Kingmaker', son-in-law of Richard Beauchamp, who became Earl in 1449. He used the bear and ragged staff of his wife's family. The Herald's College has a seal with an impression of the bear and ragged staff dating from 1454. When the Dudley family became earls of Warwick in 1547 they used the badge and Robert Dudley, Earl of Leicester, placed it in the Lord Leycester Hospital and on his tomb, and even on one of his suits of armour. The next family to take over the badge was the Greville family when they became earls of Warwick and it is still being used. The Earl of Warwick had to give permission for the County Council to adopt the bear and ragged staff. Gradually the badge came to be associated not only with the earls but with the town of Warwick and the county of Warwickshire. History does not explain why the bear was chained to the ragged staff.

The Bear and Ragged Staff.

The Court House

The Court House, a Grade I listed building and an excellent example of eighteenth-century architecture, was used as a magistrates' court until 1970, when the official body moved to Leamington Spa. The earliest surviving evidence of a building on the site comes from 1340, when Richard Aleyn gave two shops to his son William. A later owner was the Earl of Warwick, Thomas Beauchamp. By 1510 this corner site contained a timber-framed building, called the Cross Tavern because it was next to the High Cross, a place where the east–west and north–south roads met. The Parlour on the first floor, fronting on to Castle Street, was used for Corporation business, and was the only part that was damaged by the fire. By the 1720s the Corporation decided to have a new building to reflect the importance of the Town Council and to complement the quality of the houses on the three other corners. The commission was given to Francis Smith, a notable Warwick builder. He was probably influenced by the Italian architects of the day and incorporated elements of highly fashionable palazzo design. Unfortunately, it has a flat roof – not the wisest architectural feature for an English building! It was completed by 1730.

Court House.

A central niche on the Jury Street front contains a figure of Justice with the Royal Arms above and the badge of the town below. These were carved in 1731 by Thomas Stayner at a cost of £15. Unfortunately, the sword has disappeared. The statue has a secret! It was cast in metal but cleverly made to look like stone.

The Court House became the centre of fashionable life, the scene of balls, assemblies and public meetings. The Ballroom has a small musicians' gallery on its eastern wall, but since the removal of the staircase leading to it in the restoration of the 1950s, the gallery has been inaccessible. The Court House also hosted entertainment for people who attended the Assizes, Quarter Sessions, race meetings, military drilling, and other pleasurable pursuits.

The Court House remains the home of Warwick Town Council and contains the Council Chamber, the Mayor's Parlour (at present the Tourist Information Centre), the Town Clerk's Office, Assembly Rooms and a ballroom upstairs. The basement, formerly the kitchen, today accommodates the Warwickshire Yeomanry Museum. Old buildings have voracious appetites and need constant upkeep. Money is always hard to come by and the Court House interiors, although loved by the occupiers, now require renovation. The Town Council's ambition is to open the Court House to the general public and to provide a Visitor Centre where they can experience its history.

Warwick Town Council's application to the Heritage Lottery Fund was successful. This will allow extensive restoration and conservation work to be carried out on the Court House to make it more accessible to the residents of Warwick. The project will include an Interpretation Centre to tell the story of the building and to provide residents and visitors with an insight into the rich heritage of Warwick.

Ballroom.

Town Council Chamber.

Thomas Oken's Chest.

The Pageant Garden

The Pageant Garden, the garden of the Pageant House, No. 2, Jury Street, is an unexpected little haven in the centre of town. The Pageant House was owned by the Greenway family in the late eighteenth and nineteenth centuries. The Greenways gradually bought up properties behind their house so that they could create a pleasant garden, complete with a conservatory for the newly imported plants so beloved of Victorian gardeners. In 1887 the house was bought by Sir Edward Montague Nelson (a local industrialist), who later made it available to the Warwick Pageant Committee. The committee bought the house for the town in 1908, and the long association with the annual Warwick Pageant led to the present name of both house and garden.

The garden provides a small shady retreat just off Castle Street and near to the entrance to the castle. The garden is protected from the street by a hedge of yew and holly. There is a central lawn, overshadowed by two large chestnut trees, a sweet chestnut, *Castanea sativa,* and a red-flowered horse chestnut, *Aesculus x carnea Briotti.* Other interesting trees include a tulip tree, *Liriodendron tulipifera*, and several different varieties of maple including *Acer platanoides Schwedleri*, with deep red buds in winter, red young leaves and good autumn colour. There are some ornamental shrubs and roses, and a wisteria on the house wall provides colour in late spring. The garden is used for civic receptions, and is also popular for weddings.

The Pageant House and Garden.

Oken's House

Thomas Oken was a great benefactor to Warwick in the sixteenth century. His date of birth is not known but he became a merchant and by 1545 he was Master of the United Guilds, and owing to his status and business experience he became Mayor of the new Corporation. He owned several properties in the town but his home was No. 3 High Street.

The building now known as Oken's House is formed from two separate structures. The area behind the garage door, the present entrance room and the two rooms above (the one over the garage is inaccessible) would have been one dwelling house. The second dwelling, consisting of the other two ground floor rooms and two upstairs rooms and the upstairs room of the earlier house, is open to the public today. Oken rented these dwellings to tenants.

Although it looks like a gem of Tudor architecture, with its timber framing and projecting upper storey, regrettably the house has been much altered and refaced. During its long life the building has been put to many uses. In 1790 the Countess of Warwick established a School of Industry here for girls aged between eight and fourteen. The original numbers were about sixty and it must have been very crowded. The school moved to Number 9 Castle Street in 1823 and survived until 1882.

In the 1950s the building became a dolls' house! Joy Robinson, who lived in St Nicholas Park Street, wanted somewhere to display her growing private collection of dolls and toys and took on the lease of Oken's House sometime in the 1950s. When she died, her sister Peggy moved to Warwick to run the Doll Museum and then she offered the collection for sale when she wanted to retire in 1987. The Warwickshire Museum raised the money to buy the collection, and then took on the lease of Oken's House to continue displaying the collection. It was a very popular venue, attracting thousands of visitors each year.

Warwickshire Museum also used the collection for educational projects but in 2005 the museum decided to vacate Oken's House because it was a difficult building – very poor for visitors with disabilities and rather tight for school groups, which all added to the wear and tear on the building. When the lease came up for renewal it was decided not to renew. The safety of the collection was never in doubt – the collection is part of the museum's collections, and most of the dolls and toys are now in store.

Thomas Oken died in 1573 and has been remembered as a great benefactor to his town. Sadly, he and his wife had no children. His will covered every possible need, both of the people and the fabric of the town, and he was able to enrich his church.

Oken's House.

Interior.

The Friends Meeting House

Members of the Society of Friends, known as Quakers, came to Warwick in the seventeenth century and today their quiet but friendly meeting house welcomes all visitors to worship with them, enjoy the café, the garden and the friendly atmosphere. This group was founded after a visit by George Fox, founder of the Quakers, who came to Warwick in 1655 and 1656. Up to 1669 they kept no known conventicle (or assembly); however, by 1671 their presence must have been accepted and they were able to buy a house on this site. Unfortunately, it was one of the first buildings to be destroyed in the Great Fire of 1694. However, the meeting house was very quickly rebuilt in 1695 and its structure reflects the Friends' desire to keep some of the original features of brick and timber framing. The front was rendered about 1700.

Quaker Meeting House.

Quaker Meeting Room.

The group's numbers reached 250 but decline set in during the eighteenth century. In 1909 the meetings were 'laid down' (ceased) and the buildings were let out for other uses. The section at the back was used as a private dwelling, with the front section let as offices to an architect, a firm of accountants and a hairdresser.

The meeting house was reconvened and opened in 1949 and from 1954 the Friends have used the building regularly for worship. At that time the building was in poor condition so in 1990 it was refronted with the red brick visible on High Street. This now contains a café in which meals and snacks are provided by friendly staff.

The Friends Meeting House is available for hire, and provides a restful, congenial environment for talks, concerts, meetings, Quaker weddings and choir practices.

The Garden of the Friends Meeting House

Behind the Friends' Meeting House is a small, quiet and intimate garden. The house was once the home of some of the first Quakers to live in Warwick, and the garden was originally their burial ground. It has not been used for this purpose for many years, though there are two small twentieth-century memorial plaques to be seen. There are two entrances, a rather grand one off the High Street, approached through an archway with 'Friends Meeting House' inscribed on it, and a wooden door at the far end which leads into the garden from Castle Lane, just north of Leycester Place. Near the doorway to the Meeting House is a large old stone well, now empty but obviously once used to provide the water supply for the house.

The area of the garden is not large; it is only about 50 metres long by 25 metres wide at its widest point, but it forms a secluded and quite private place, enclosed by walls and in addition, to the north, by three fine mature trees, a birch, a medlar and a mulberry tree. Medlars and mulberries were often planted in gardens in past

The Garden of the Friends Meeting House.

centuries, and these trees fruit well in favourable years when the summer rainfall is greater than usual. There is a small avenue of clipped yews to the south of the garden, underplanted very successfully with variegated ground elder, which does not spread like the plain green variety. In the lawn adjacent to this avenue there is a small path made of slabs set in the grass. The path and the variegated ground elder were among improvements added to the garden some twenty years ago. At the end of this avenue there is a bench and a table, and there are other benches which overlook the lawn with a view of the castle beyond. Planting is very simple: ornamental shrubs and climbers together with herbaceous plants and a little bedding, which together provide some colour for most of the year.

The garden of the Friends Meeting House, the yew hedge underplanted with variegated ground elder.

Lord Leycester Hospital

This magnificent complex of buildings rivals the castle for being the most well-known and photographed building in Warwick. Part of it includes the Chapel of St James, which is sited over the Westgate, first mentioned in 1123. After falling into disrepair it was rebuilt in 1383 and gifted by Richard II to the Guild of St George. The Guild of Holy Trinity and the Blessed Virgin also moved to the site and by 1413 the two guilds had been combined into the United Guilds. The two guilds were dissolved in 1546 as a result of the Reformation.

Charities and acts of public piety were certain to enhance the reputation of their founders, and Robert Dudley, Earl of Leicester, was not a man to miss such a chance. He had plans to establish a hospital for the poor either in Warwick or nearby and had already obtained a licence by an act of Parliament. (The word 'hospital' is used in its ancient sense, meaning 'a charitable institution for the housing and maintenance of the needy, infirm or aged'.) Despite Dudley's charitable intention he was not universally admired. In 1571 he visited Warwick to celebrate his investiture as a member of the Order of St Michael, an honour awarded by the French king. The bailiffs and burgesses had decided not to welcome Dudley and his large party of aristocrats and court officials formally when they arrived at Warwick. The bailiffs said the earl and his visitors were only subjects of the Queen, and did not rate a royal welcome.

Dudley was highly offended and refused to speak to them when they called on him the next day. The burgesses craved his pardon and Dudley accepted, with a warning to them that in future they should behave more dutifully. Before Dudley left Warwick he looked at some possible sites for his hospital, one of which was a plot at St Mary's church but this proved unsuitable. At this point the dubious action of one John Butler played into his hands. He was one of the principal burgesses and was also one of Dudley's servants. Either in secret agreement with Dudley or in an attempt to please him, Butler informed him that the Corporation would be prepared to donate its Guild Hall. This was news to the other burgesses but, unwilling to aggravate Dudley again, they transferred the site to the earl on 26 December 1571.

The hospital was to provide homes for twelve old and infirm soldiers or seamen and their wives. The men were called Brethren and were overseen by a master and it was run on the terms of the original charter until 1956. Dudley created a book of ordinances, statutes, and rules for his hospital which clearly spelt out the strict lines on how it was to be run. The present Master's favourite is No. 22 (relating to laundresses):

> Item – That no Brother take any woman to serve or tend upon him in his chamber without special licence of the Master, nor any with licence, under the age of three-score years, except she be his wife, mother, sister, or daughter, upon the pains last mentioned for their several offence.

The charter was then updated, but the purpose of the Lord Leycester Hospital is still accommodation and today eight ex-servicemen and their wives live in more modern and comfortable lodgings. They attend services in the chapel every weekday except Monday. Above the gateway there are two shields – on the left the green two-tailed lion of the

Lord Leycester Hospital.

Great Hall.

Dudley family and on the right the De L'Isle arms, a title held by Robert Dudley's brother Ambrose, Earl of Warwick. The present Viscount De L'Isle is the patron of the Hospital.

Until the twentieth century the buildings to the right of the hospital's gate were not part of the hospital. The building next door, the former Anchor Inn, is one of the most important of the surviving sixteenth-century buildings in the town. The timber, brickwork and muted colour of the hospital are fine examples of what other buildings in Warwick may have looked like before the Victorians painted them black and white.

There are three halls in the hospital. One is the magnificent Great Hall, which is frequently used for concerts and is for hire by private parties. Upstairs from the courtyard is the Guild Hall, the site of which was granted to the burgesses in 1393 and built by Richard Neville, Earl of Warwick, known as 'The Kingmaker'. This was the private chamber where the Guilds met. The table is original and King James I used the chair when he dined in the Great Hall in 1617. Until the 1950s the hall was divided into cubicles, providing the sleeping quarters for the Brethren. Part of the Guild Hall and the small hall are home to the museum of the local Warwickshire cavalry regiment, the Queen's Own Hussars, first raised in 1685.

Food was cooked for the Brethren on the ground floor and the kitchen is still in use, now offering meals and snacks to visitors. Robert Dudley's presence is still apparent in his initials on the fireplace. The Brethren too are a constant reminder of his provision. Part of the agreement when taking up accommodation is that the Brethren perform light duties. These include acting as guides to visitors and running the small but well-appointed shop so that, as well as being provided with a home, they are also part of a community, valued for their service to the country.

Although Robert Dudley has not always enjoyed a good reputation, his action in founding the Lord Leycester Hospital has been an unquestioned benefit to Warwick, its people and the many retired servicemen and their wives who have lived here.

The Master's House.

Courtyard.

Guild Hall.

St James's Chapel.

Lord Leycester Hospital Gardens

There are two gardens at the Lord Leycester Hospital: a small modern knot garden known as the Millennium Knot Garden, which is immediately behind the buildings, and the main garden further to the rear of the property. The main garden is accessible through the Knot Garden and also through the entrance arch from the car park.

The Millennium Knot Garden, created predominantly in boxwood, was designed to echo the pattern of the timbering on the old building adjacent to it. A large statue of the Bear and Ragged Staff, the emblem of the earls of Warwick, has been placed in this garden. Designed by Rachel Higgins, this symbolic memorial statue was created in 1998. Various aspects of the statue represent parts of the hospital, such as the medieval St James's Chapel on Westgate where the Brethren worship, and the uniform of the Queen's Own Hussars, the museum of which is housed within the hospital buildings.

The main garden, which was always part of the original site, and is therefore now more than four hundred years old, is divided into two parts. That nearest to the hospital and adjoining the Master's house is a private garden for the use of the Master. It is separated

The Millennium Garden, showing ornamental timbering on the building. The pattern is repeated in the design of the clipped boxwood planting below.

by a hornbeam hedge from the other half of the garden, where the Brethren could grow their own vegetables. The hedge is dissected by a path, and within the hedge line there is a medieval Norman arch, thought to be the old chancel arch from St James's Chapel. The chapel had been restored in 1808–10 by a pupil of Gilbert Scott when it was discovered to be in danger of falling down. Framed by the arch is a great sandstone vase-shaped structure, more than 2,000 years old, thought to have originally graced the top of a Nileometer, one of many columns built by the Romans to measure the height of the Nile in flood. It was donated to the garden by the Earl of Warwick in 1838.

The Restoration of the Master's Garden

By the end of the twentieth century much of the Master's Garden had fallen into disrepair, and it had been closed to the public for more than a hundred years. Following research carried out in the 1990s by garden historian Susan Rhodes, the wife of the then Master, Captain Dermot Rhodes, it was realised that the garden had been a popular tourist venue in Victorian times. The American writer Nathaniel Hawthorn had commented favourably on the garden following his visit, writing in 1857 that 'Each brother has a little garden of his own, and the master has, also, a nice garden. There is a beautiful little thatched summerhouse where they can go and sit in warm weather, smoke their pipes, muse over the past, and play at chess or checkers.'

A plan of the Master's Garden made in 1851 for the local Board of Health revealed the layout to be substantially similar to that which still remained at the end of the twentieth century. The far part of the garden was divided into two sections lined with trees, most probably fruit trees. A ring of cobbles, about 11 feet in diameter but below the present ground level, was found during excavations, and was identified as the site of a summerhouse, though all trace of the building itself had vanished. Behind the summerhouse there was a greenhouse. In the corner of the brick wall enclosing the garden on the north and east sides stood the remains of a small two-storey brick building, obviously constructed as a gazebo and dating probably from the seventeenth century. Adjacent to the gazebo, an exciting discovery was made – the remains of an eighteenth-century pinery, or hotbed, for the production of pineapples.

A decision was made to try to raise enough money to carry out a complete restoration, and a substantial grant was given to the project by the local King Henry VIII Endowed Trust. That, together with numerous other donations, including money raised by sales of a Millennium plate illustrating scenes of Warwick and designed by Christine Measures, provided funds to finance the work. The inspiration behind both the Millennium Garden and the restoration work for the Master's Garden was the work of Susan Rhodes together with Geoffrey Smith, a Warwick landscape architect and committee member of the Warwickshire Gardens Trust. The actual garden plans for the summerhouse, the gazebo and the garden layout were created by Geoffrey Smith. Members of the Trust provided practical volunteer work and also gifts of suitable plant material for replanting the ornamental flower beds. A new circular summerhouse with a thatched conical roof was constructed at the end of the central path, copying that found in an old photograph. The gazebo was redesigned, leaving an open ground-floor area for horticultural requirements

Above left: The Master's Garden, the path leading from the summerhouse to the Nileometer 'vase'.

Above right: The Master's Garden, the Nileometer 'vase', with the arch just visible in the hedge behind.

Right: The Master's Garden, a view showing the gazebo behind the lawn.

and storage. A wooden staircase now leads up to the second floor, where a small room houses an exhibition on the restoration of the garden. There is a fine view west from the top of the staircase over the old town wall and the town and countryside beyond, and the gazebo itself is a delightful little building.

The old pineapple pit still has the remains of its underfloor heating system or hypocaust, which was fed by pipes from a brick stove. The growing of pineapples was a fashionable craze in the eighteenth century. The plants, which were probably obtained from the pinery at Warwick Castle, took two years to mature and fruit. They were grown in frames on beds of fermenting tanning bark (a waste product from the tanning of leather) which had to be kept at a minimum temperature of 70° F throughout for the successful production of fruit, no easy task in the fluctuating temperatures of the English climate.

The greenhouse has been restored. The western section of the garden has been divided into quarters where vegetables are grown. The cross paths, which meet at a central sundial, have been laid with brick in a herringbone pattern. A new lawn was laid in the eastern half of the garden, and iron rose arches, made by the Warwick blacksmith George Worrall to match the old ones, now support rambler roses and clematis down the central pathway. Topiary figures in box, together with ornamental planting and specimen trees complete the garden plan.

Having had a number of years to mature, the restored garden is now a most attractive and interesting place to visit, not only for its planting and its historical associations, but also for the satisfying appearance of rows of healthy vegetables, all used for meals in the hospital.

The Master's Garden, an old wooden wheelbarrow by the vegetable plots.

Hill Close Gardens Centre

Many of the people who lived in the tightly packed centre of Warwick did not have gardens. Hill Close Gardens were created in the latter half of the nineteenth century to provide individual plots for these people to rent or buy in order to make gardens. These were successful but later fell into disuse and by the 1990s few people even realised that they once existed. The gardens were rediscovered in 1993 and local residents organised a study of options to secure their future. This led in 2000 to the foundation of a charitable trust. A team of volunteers then set to work to restore them and open the Gardens to the public.

It became apparent that a significant building was needed to accommodate the visitors, volunteers, schoolchildren and staff. Offices, refreshment and toilet facilities, study areas and archive storage were essential. Work in the gardens, including use of the site by groups such as clubs, schools, business and private hirers, required the generation of revenue while the gardens were being brought back to their former glory.

Warwickshire County Council lent the Gardens Trust a temporary building while the trustees planned a suitable permanent centre. The architectural style was most important. Should it be in keeping with the Victorian image of the garden or be a modern building and, if so, what style? Three companies were shortlisted and Design Engine won the

Newest building – Hill Close Centre.

contract. A daring decision had been taken to go ultra-modern! The company had taken into consideration the damp, boggy area where they could build without compromising the historicity of the site.

Plans had to include views of the garden, plenty of interior light, storage, office and kitchen space as well as addressing the needs of external hirers. The building also was required to fulfil the twenty-first-century standards of sustainability.

Thanks to a successful lottery bid and grants and donations, these plans could be realised and work commenced in 2006. Hill Close Garden Centre was opened to the public in 2007 and the result is an acclaimed success – a single-storey triangular building with a flat roof, two walls of glass and the third of tiles. The frame is parallam – reconstituted timber made of chippings and glue pressed together. Instead of wattle and daub, the infill is shredded newspaper blown behind fixed plasterboard. Interestingly, the construction is very similar to medieval timber-framed houses, of which Warwick has some good examples. The terracotta tiles provide cladding against the rain and the warm colour is in harmony with the terracotta flower pots and the Victorian summerhouses. The roof is perfectly designed to suit its garden environment. Living sedum planted on a special waterproof material provides insulation to keep the building warm in winter and cool in summer, absorbing rainwater and gradually releasing it to the storm drains. The building is heated by a ground source heat pump – another use of modern technology.

The interior is bright and cheerful, spacious and functional. It is a popular venue for group activities, including talks, lectures, conferences, school visits, open days and special events. The kitchen provides sufficient facilities to produce cooked meals so private parties can hire the centre. Books, cards and other garden-related products are on sale. The Victorian Gardens and its modern Centre are a successful combination of the old and the new.

HCC Meeting Room.

Hill Close Gardens

Hill Close Gardens are a group of small gardens on the hill overlooking the racecourse in Warwick. They date from 1845, when the owner of the original pasture decided to divide his land up into small gardens to rent out. The gardens represent a remarkable survival of Victorian 'detached gardens', or gardens which have no house attached to them. They were originally created for residents of the town, as many people, from master craftsmen to businessmen and professionals, lived 'above the shop' with only a small yard behind the house for workshops, washhouses, privies, and perhaps a stable for the horse and delivery van. Similar gardens had once existed to the north of the town, and also around many other towns and cities, for example in Cheylesmore Park, in Coventry, where the gardens had been started around 1800. Nearly all of these garden sites have since been built on, however, and Hill Close Gardens are thought to be one of only four such sites remaining in the whole country.

In the mid-nineteenth century most people were not rich enough to own a carriage and therefore the means of getting out of town. The plots at Hill Close therefore offered a valuable means of escape and healthy recreation, providing a little area of garden which could be used both to grow vegetables and fruit trees, and also a small ornamental lawn. The view out from the site to the west was attractive, looking over the adjacent racecourse which encircled the Common. Racing had begun at Warwick in 1707, and the race meetings were always popular events.

At first the new gardens were tenanted, but tenants became interested in owning their plots, and permanent structures such as little summerhouses, some even with fireplaces, were built. By the end of the nineteenth century many of the gardens had been bought outright. Families often carried on their ownership for several generations; one example is the Margetts family of local auctioneers and surveyors, whose family firm was started in 1806. John Margetts organised the surveying and sale of the gardens in 1865, and rented one of the plots himself, although he actually lived in a Georgian house with its own garden in the town. His garden plot was eventually bought by his grandson, and the family continued to use the garden until 1981. The Margetts' plot, No. 10, has a deep well in one corner, to which all the gardeners had access.

The Chadbands were another local family who were associated with the gardens for many years. Benjamin Chadband ran a business based on pork, pork pies and also confectionery. He took a plot in 1870 which he subsequently bought in 1873, where as well as gardening, he kept pigs in a pigsty. He also kept pigs in an adjacent area known as Bread and Meat Close. The keeping of pigs became quite popular with owners and tenants, and some of the brick-built pigsties are still there. Keeping a pig, which was fed largely on household scraps, provided a useful and inexpensive source of meat for the family. Slaughtering would take place in the autumn and early winter months, the times being staggered so that neighbours could be given a joint of meat in exchange for one of theirs later on. The sides of bacon would be prepared by being cured in saltpetre, and

Hill Close Gardens, one of the restored summerhouses.

then smoked. The Chadband family kept their garden plot on until 1981, and ran their pork business well into the twentieth century. The shop continued to specialise in pork products until 2006, though by this date it was in different ownership.

During the twentieth century the effects of two World Wars began to take their toll, and after the Second World War the gardens became more and more abandoned. The whole garden area, except for two plots which were still tenanted and used as vegetable gardens, gradually became a complete wilderness of elder, brambles, ivy, overgrown privet hedges and self-set trees. The summerhouses were still there, but could only be seen at all if you pushed through the undergrowth and peered under the encroaching ivy and through the broken panes of the windows. Warwick District Council had planned to redevelop the site for housing, and it was only when they began practical site investigations in 1993 that locals became concerned by what might be about to happen to the site. The thought of council houses worried the nearby residents, who asked various organisations, including the Warwickshire Gardens Trust, if they could help to investigate the history and possible importance of the site. The Trust had recently been set up to research and to record the county's gardens and parks, and raise public awareness of the importance of our historic gardens.

Hill Close Gardens, a shady corner in one of the gardens. Note the Victorian edging tiles at the front of the picture.

Research into the site at Hill Close carried out by local historian Christine Hodgetts, one of the founder members of the Trust, revealed a plan which had been published by the Warwick Board of Health in 1851 showing the layout of the gardens. Hedges divided the plots; there were individual path layouts within each, and even the positions of fruit trees were marked. Several plots were shown with their own summerhouses. This plan provided incontrovertible proof of the historic value of the gardens and their existence since the mid-nineteenth century. Following the successful application to English Heritage to have the whole of the Hill Close site at Warwick listed, the Council dropped their plans for housing and backed the restoration plans. A trust was set up to administer everything, and in 2006 work began. The project has been financially assisted by a grant from the Heritage Lottery Fund as well as numerous donations by local charitable organisations.

In restoring the gardens, the aim has been to retain the old outlines, with the features which can be identified from the 1851 map. These include the little summerhouses, the sites of the fruit trees, many of which are still growing, the internal garden paths, and the hedges and paths which divide one plot from another and provide access. The original plot numbers have been retained, though these are not always consecutive since some of the gardens have been lost in the past to building. Traditional materials have been used as far as possible, when still available, and health and safety regulations have intervened in some cases, since the gardens are now open to the public. The garden plots varied in both size and layout, reflecting the aspirations and finances of their owners. Archaeological investigations were carried out prior to the restoration of the plots, revealing some interesting facts, including the original construction of some of the garden steps, and the materials used for the paths. The latter were mainly of ash and clinker, probably a cheap by-product from the local gasworks near the Common.

A volunteer team began work on the gardens, which were later, in 1998, opened occasionally to the public. A portable unit was brought in to allow schools to make regular educational visits. The problem of maintenance was gradually solved by the newly renovated plots being offered to individuals and organisations who would take them on. Plot 24, now tended by George Mills, is the only plot which has been in continual cultivation from the mid-nineteenth century, and Mr Mills has worked it since before the land was originally sold to the Council. Various local people who have insufficient garden space of their own in Warwick, and organisations such as Plant Heritage, formerly known as the NCCPG (National Council for the Conservation of Plants and Gardens), now cultivate the plots, retaining the original layouts and looking after the remaining old fruit trees.

Plant Heritage grows decorative varieties of plants at risk of disappearing from cultivation, and on other plots only those flowering plants which would have been available to the Victorians are grown. Most people continue to grow a mix of ornamental plants and vegetables, as has been the case since the gardens' inception. The old apple varieties have largely been identified through the painstaking work of the late Noreen Jardine, and are now all labelled. The growing of fruit, particularly apples, was very popular. Some locally raised varieties which had been planted in the gardens include the dessert apple Blenheim Orange, originally found as a seedling at Blenheim Park in Oxfordshire in the mid-eighteenth century; Bramley's seedling, raised in a cottage garden in Nottinghamshire about 1810; the Warwickshire variety Wyken Pippin; and

Hill Close Gardens, a colourful border with the tiled roof of another summerhouse showing behind.

Above left: Hill Close Gardens, a productive vegetable garden.

Above right: Hill Close Gardens, an old pear tree carrying a good crop of fruit.

the yellow plum Warwickshire Drooper, so called because of the tree's drooping growth habit.

One of the outstanding features of interest in the gardens is the number of little summerhouses which have been discovered and restored. The finest one is, unfortunately, in one of the two top gardens on the hillside which are now in private ownership, having been built previously on land which was part of the site of the old Bowling Green Inn. This brick summerhouse has a pitched roof with decorative tiling, a glazed front door and matching sash windows. Inside there is a small fireplace. There are two listed hexagonal summerhouses on the main site dating from before 1866, one of which, on Plot 19, has windows which were made to the pattern of the original from remains found in rubbish near the building. The first owner of this plot kept the White Swan in Brook Street. In the twentieth century the plot was used to grow produce for a greengrocer's shop in Market Place. One or two of the summerhouses have carved bargeboards under the eaves, a decorative feature which is typical of many older Warwickshire houses. Old gardening tools are kept in some of the little houses, and visitors can go inside one or two.

A great deal of thought, enthusiasm, and hard work has gone into the remarkable resurrection and renovation of Hill Close Gardens.

Hill Close Gardens, a view over the gardens with the Common in the background.

Warwick Common

The Common, tucked away on the western edge of town, is Warwick's oldest recreational area. Historically, the people of Warwick have had access to the common since at least the early thirteenth century, when the right to graze horses and cattle, two animals per house, was granted to householders. This right was only abolished in 1948, when Warwick Corporation took over the control of the land. Besides grazing rights, the common was traditionally used for sports and as a military training ground.

In 1707 Warwick Racecourse was first laid out around the common, and Lord Brooke himself gave money 'towards making a horse race'. The races, run over fences, still take place several times a year, attracting enthusiastic racegoers from local people to county gentry. There is all the razzmatazz associated with a race meeting: betting stands, sideshows and refreshment stalls. The Tattersalls grandstand is probably the oldest in the country.

Today the common is managed for its wildlife interest. No weedkillers or fertilisers have been used on the grass, where larks nest in the spring and wildflowers grow. Even the occasional autumn crocus, probably *Crocus speciosus*, can sometimes be found. Autumn crocuses were grown here in the fifteenth century for their anthers (part of the flower) which were used as a substitute for saffron in cooking. The real saffron crocus, *Crocus sativus*, is grown mainly in Mediterranean countries such as Morocco, since it requires hot summer conditions to ripen the corm.

There is a caravan site on the common and golf is also available.

Racing at Warwick.

The Priory

Warwick Priory has, for most of its life, been a mystery to the people of Warwick as a feeling of separation developed between its owners and the town. It began its long existence as a monastic establishment and then a private dwelling, comfortable and lavished with attention. Its fortunes then declined. The building went through periods of neglect and finally was ignominiously deconstructed and most of the materials were shipped to foreign lands. Sadly little remains of this once most magnificent edifice but the present building is just as important as the one it has replaced.

The Priory was founded as the Priory of St Sepulchre by Henry de Beaumont, first Earl of Warwick, between 1114 and 1119. It belonged to the Order of the Canon of the Holy Sepulchre, who had the special duty of caring for pilgrims to the Holy Land. These canons were distinguished by a double red cross on the breast of their habit. After the fall of Jerusalem in 1188, the house became indistinguishable from an ordinary Augustinian priory. There were eight canons besides the prior in 1339. The

The Priory *c.* 1800.

end of its life as a priory came with Henry VIII's reforms, and the incumbent prior, Robert Radford, was forced to surrender the house to the Crown, and was retired with a pension of £5.

Thomas Hawkins (otherwise known as Fisher) was granted the Priory in 1546. By reputation the son of a Warwick fishmonger, he went into the service of the Duke of Somerset. He then moved to the household of John Dudley, who became the Earl of Warwick in 1547 and later Duke of Northumberland, the father-in-law of Lady Jane Grey. Fisher gradually accumulated a substantial estate of lands formerly belonging to the Church. Sir William Dugdale, the Warwickshire antiquary, recorded that:

> he pull'd to the ground this Monastery and raised in the place of it a very fair House ... which, being finished about the 8. year of Queen Eliz. Reign, he made his principall seat, giving it a new name (somewhat alluding to his own),viz: Hawkyns Nest, or Hawks Nest, by reason of its situation, having a pleasant grove of loftie elmes almost environing it.

The new house was finished in 1566 and although it is not clear what it looked like it was probably built round a courtyard. In 1572 Queen Elizabeth paid Mr Fisher a surprise visit, which no doubt cost him a large sum of money. Unfortunately, after his death in 1577 his eldest son, Edward, wasted his inheritance and in 1581 sold the Priory to John Puckering who enjoyed living in the very fair house, in contrast to the profligate Edward, who ended his days in the Fleet Prison. Puckering was a lawyer who became Speaker of the House of Commons, and was made Keeper of the Great Seal in 1592 and knighted. It was probably he who rebuilt the hall range of the original house in the 1590s. This was elaborately decorated with strapwork ornament placed over the bay windows and a row of six curved gables crowning the roofline. These features were popular in Warwickshire houses of the time and can be seen on the slightly later St John's House in Coten End.

His son, Thomas, thankfully an ideal heir, succeeded his father in 1596, and was made a baronet in 1612. It is believed that he was responsible for building the east range in the 1620s or 1630s, and for making many other alterations to the house and grounds: the form of the house was little altered during the next 300 years.

'Make-overs' are not new! Sir Thomas spent lavishly on fashionable features and it was probably during his occupancy that the house reached its architectural zenith. Inside there was a finely carved oak staircase which led to the Great Chamber and a gallery where, in 1737, George Vertue, the antiquarian, noted there hung a collection of portraits of 'great, Learned remarkable men in Europe'. The rooms were richly decorated and Sir Thomas's wealth was reflected in the Hearth Tax returns of 1663, which showed that he had thirty-six hearths. This made the house one of the largest in the county.

Like many families of that time, the male line ran out after the death of Sir Thomas in 1636. The house passed to his daughter, then to a cousin, Sir Henry Newton, who took the name Puckering. He represented Warwickshire in Parliament from 1661 to 1669, and when not carrying out these duties he may have laid out the formal gardens shown in the view in 1711. He died in 1700 and the Priory was inherited by his niece, who sold the estate to Henry Wise, the Warwickshire-born gardener. However, the niece's dowager

Priory – foundations.

Priory wall.

rights allowed her to live in the property for life and, unfortunately for Mr Wise, she lived for many years and he was not able to move in until 1727.

Henry Wise enjoyed only ten years at the Priory, and after his death in 1737 the house was lived in by the family for three generations until 1805. It was at this time that the Priory's fortunes began their downward spiral. The owners appeared to lose interest in living there and it was leased out to a succession of tenants with long periods when it was not occupied. By the time Henry Christopher Wise inherited in 1850, the railway was about to come to Warwick. The route was planned to cut through the North Park, just by the house, and would cut across the Priory Pools, thus dividing the estate in two. Naturally the family did not wish to live in the house and in 1851 the Priory and 37 acres of adjoining land were sold to the Birmingham and Oxford Junction Railway Company.

The railway was opened on 1 October 1852. The house, gardens and pleasure grounds were left unoccupied and were sold to William Scott in 1863. Thomas Lloyd, a member of the famous Birmingham banking family, bought it in 1865 and gradually bought back parts of the Priory grounds not sold to the railway company. By 1889 he had acquired the whole of the Priory estate south of the railway line. It seemed that the house had attracted good fortune once again. Lloyd spent a lot of money on extensive alterations and additional outbuildings, such as a new stable and coach house.

However, after Lloyd's death in 1890 the house's future once again looked uncertain. Various family members lived there but finally moved out in 1902. Robert Emmett, a wealthy American, leased the house until 1907, after which it remained empty until 1910. The family then tried to sell the property but it was withdrawn from the auction and Thomas Owen Lloyd, a relative of the earlier Thomas, took up residence. In 1918 he offered the Priory as a residence to the bishop of the new diocese of Coventry – this would have been full circle, taken into the care of a religious body. But it was not to be – the offer was declined. The family remained there until 1921 then moved to Budbrook House. The Priory had reached the end of its long and distinguished life.

In 1925 two demolition sales were held in July and September. Alexander Weddell, an American diplomat, bought the shell of the building and had it transported to Virginia, America, where it was reconstructed and called Virginia House. It was not a faithful reconstruction of the Priory but it did retain its essential features. Among the ensuing local and national controversy, Alexander Weddell explained the purchase of the Priory in a published interview from 1925:

Before we had even heard of Warwick Priory, and before our arrival in England, the old place had begun to be stripped of practically everything – stairs, flooring, paneling, ironwork, guttering, roofing, etc. – and the empty shell was announced for sale at auction in September ... It is not our purpose to attempt to reconstruct the Priory in America, but it has seemed to us that the use of the stone and brick from this old place, material with the bloom of centuries upon it, would not be inappropriate for a structure which will become eventually in the nature of a public monument, housing an institution – the Virginia Historical Society – which has for many years been a guardian of historical treasures in Virginia ...

The estate and the remaining buildings were left to stand empty until acquired by Warwickshire County Council in 1939 but plans for development had to be postponed because of the war. In 1953 the park was opened to the public. After this, excavations were carried out which revealed much of the history of the site.

In 1973 Warwickshire County Council built a free-standing modern structure to house the historical records of Warwickshire. These had been the subject of discussion since 1931, when the council appointed a Records Committee to consider how the records should be cared for and made available to the public. Deposits began to arrive from 1933 under the care of a professional archivist and these were stored in spare rooms in Shire Hall. After the Second World War the collection grew, so more basement rooms had to be converted to strong rooms and more staff required desk space. The decision was taken to create a purpose-built office. The new record office was officially opened on 23 March 1974. History has always been a popular subject and the office was busy but the enthusiasm for family history research in the 1970s led to huge increases in visitor levels. By the late 1990s it was obvious that expansion was necessary. As a result of a successful Lottery Bid for £1.4 million, the building was refurbished and extended in 2002/03, with two new strong rooms and improved

The Cottage.

Demolition 1925.

facilities for researchers. There is also a readers' tea room and opportunities to buy books and other items.

A reminder of the old Priory is still visible in an adjacent building, called 'the Bungalow', which now houses the conservation workshop. A cottage attached to this building was part of the original Priory. It has been refurbished as offices and is awaiting occupation. One last indication of an historic site is a small section to the right of the main entrance where archaeologists have preserved a part of the foundations of the original monastic building.

Although there is little left of the Priory, it is fit and proper that Warwickshire's priceless archives are deposited and cared for on the site of one of Warwick's most important and historic buildings.

Warwickshire County Record Office.

Search Room.

Priory Park

Priory Park is a large, open grassy area with many mature trees which is, surprisingly, situated near the centre of the town. It owes its position to the fact that it is all that remains of Warwick Priory, a house built on the site of the old monastic priory following the dissolution of the monasteries. In 1581 the estate was sold to John, later Sir John Puckering, keeper of the Great Seal of England. In 1596 his son Sir Thomas inherited the estate. He set about creating a garden suitable for entertaining important guests, for besides his position at Court he was also a friend of Prince Henry, Prince of Wales. The new garden had a raised terrace walk and ornamental rails with posts which were probably topped by carved heraldic beasts similar to those in contemporary royal gardens such as at Nonsuch, at Richmond and at the Great Garden, Whitehall. Sir Thomas's garden would have had parterres, or formal flowerbeds of intricate designs, to be admired from above by visitors walking along the raised terraces.

To the north of the house there were fishponds, dating from the time when the Priory was a religious house. One of these contained an island on which was built a banqueting house. This may have been interesting architecturally, since there is a record of a family visit by the Puckerings to Campden House at Chipping Campden in Gloucestershire, now known as Old Campden House, to see the banqueting houses there. These were two small buildings which matched the architectural details of the house. (Old Campden House was destroyed in the Civil War, but both of the banqueting houses have been restored as holiday homes by the Landmark Trust.) The area where the fishponds used to be was unfortunately largely destroyed when the railway was constructed in the 1850s.

Above left: Priory Park, the outline of the old garden terracing still visible in the Park.

Above right: Priory Park, a large old tree in the park, perhaps dating from the eighteenth-century planting.

In 1709 the estate was sold to Henry Wise. Wise came from an old Warwickshire family, and became gardener to Queen Anne. A map of 1711 is the earliest visual record we have of the Priory. This shows the house, the terraced walk and the parterres. By this date the parterres had been simplified to plain grass plats bordered with small clipped evergreens. Charles Bridgeman, the early eighteenth-century designer, prepared a survey of Warwick together with Henry Wise at this time, so it is possible that the two men collaborated on the laying out of the gardens and also on the planting of the trees in the Park. There is a painting by Canaletto which shows the new parterres and the view out towards the castle and the church. Canaletto painted a number of scenes of Warwick Castle and the town for Lord Brooke in the 1750s.

After the Priory was sold the gardens fell into complete disrepair and today only a few remnants of the old terraces can still be seen, although some excavations carried out in 1937 revealed the foundations of a wall, presumed to be that supporting the raised terrace walk, with steps which led up from the garden below. The Park has remained as an attractive green space in the centre of town, with magnificent mature trees. It is open at all times and regularly used by local people. An arboretum of young trees has been planted on the lower eastern part of the park, and there is quite an interesting range of native flora in the old turf, which has never been subjected to modern weedkillers and fertiliser.

Priory Park, a view of St Mary's church tower seen from within the Park.

The Old Shire Hall

For several centuries the buildings on this site were the administrative centre for law and order in Warwickshire. Sometime before 1576 the Earl of Warwick's steward lived in a house known as the Steward's Place on this site, which was then granted by the earl to the town of Warwick. It was used to administer county affairs, which included the Assize and Sheriff's courts, and from 1554 was called the Shire Hall. It was probably rebuilt in 1580/88.

The town sold the Shire Hall to the county authorities in 1675, although it was used by the town for the election of MPs, Quarter Sessions and for the meeting of the manorial court. The Hall was rebuilt between 1676 and 1680, supervised by William Hurlbutt, a Warwick architect responsible for several other buildings in the town. The Shire Hall suffered little damage in the Great Fire of 1694, possibly because it was solidly built. Efforts were made to keep it in good repair but by 1740 its condition was causing concern. In 1742 William Smith, the son of Warwick's great master builder, Francis, was asked to inspect the building and quote for repairs. He carried out some repairs in 1742 but there followed another order for another view and contract in 1744.

In 1676 all the important people of the town had ordered the erection of a new Shire Hall but it was very different in 1749 when it was proposed to rebuild yet another Shire Hall. Very few people appear to have been consulted. One who was involved was Sir Roger Newdigate of Arbury, who noted in his diary that he was going to Warwick with Francis Stratford of Merevale, to a meeting for rebuilding the Shire Hall. He subscribed ten guineas. He also noted that all the lawyers there declared that the Trustees had no power to interfere in any determination of a general meeting to repair or rebuild.

It appears that the idea of building a new hall had been agreed by various members of Warwickshire gentry rather than the traditional Quarter Sessions. Among this group there were several powerful men such as Lord Brooke from the Castle, Sir Charles Mordaunt of Walton Hall and Lord Guernsey of Packington. Friendship and a keen interest in architecture linked this group and it could be said that they forced the rebuilding when it was not strictly necessary. Their great advantage was that Sanderson Miller, squire of Radway, one of the gentry and a close friend of the group, was also one of the best-known amateur architects of the mid-eighteenth century. This connection was no doubt influential in the decision to rebuild. Another point in his favour was that he never accepted fees and his work was mostly done for friends. However, public support for the rebuilding was lukewarm and the subscription did not raise the required monies. The shortfall had to be made up by the interested gentry. The Shire Hall was rebuilt in the late 1750s to Miller's design of c. 1753.

The building was altered and repaired several times during the next centuries. Originally, the two courtrooms were open to view from the main hall but were closed off in 1780. In

Old Shire Hall.

Entrance Hall.

the 1840s the stone floor was replaced with wood and gas lighting replaced oil lamps. In 1948 the exterior stonework had deteriorated to the point of danger so it was refaced in Hollington Stone, which is much harder wearing. At this point the County Council's coat of arms was added to the pediment above the entrance.

Although the Shire Hall is one of the most important public buildings in Warwick, few members of the public have entered its grand doorway or explored its many rooms. Those who did cross the threshold were on one or other side of the law. The building's finer points of architecture and its historical significance would be far from their thoughts. The Shire Hall had been home to Warwick Assizes from the late fifteenth century until 1972, when the justice system was reorganised to be replaced by the Crown Court. By 2010 it was obvious that the eighteenth-century courts and offices were too small for today's justice system. Implementation of high-tech audio and visual systems and the extra space necessary to run a modern trial would damage the fabric of this Grade I listed building. The Court Service had to find new modern premises. On 30 December 2010 the Court Service quitted the Shire Hall to take up residence in new premises in Leamington Spa. The only formal activity that will take place in the court room in the future is the inauguration of the High Sheriff of Warwickshire.

Since then the Shire Hall has been empty and the Council faces a great challenge in making the best use of the building and obtaining sufficient income from it. Although

Entrance to Court Number One.

Court Number One.

most of the building has an air of faded elegance, there is a great deal of potential. Some rooms are well decorated and are still used for Council functions. The Judge's Dining Room is very grand and would need little refurbishment before it could be hired for public functions. However, there is much work to do to bring the main hall and the three courts up to modern safety standards. Many ideas are being considered, such as educational projects on justice, crime and punishment. School visits, tours, historical re-enactments and similar schemes have great possibilities, as well as suggestions for all types of hospitality, including weddings and concerts. Guided tours should prove very popular, especially those that take visitors on the atmospheric walk from the dock, down the narrow stairs, to a labyrinth of low-ceilinged corridors. There they would spy into the holding cells (very claustrophobic), the waiting areas and one very narrow, windowless cell where the accused was pushed in through one door to crouch until he was hauled out for trial from the other. Children would love the experience!

Ceiling in Court Number One.

Judge's Dining Room.

Old cell door.

Entrance to dungeon cell.

The herons at Shire Hall.

The New Shire Hall

This is one of the few modern buildings in the centre of Warwick and is the headquarters of Warwickshire County Council. The Shire Hall was designed by Eric Davies, then County Architect, built in 1966 and opened by the late Queen Mother. It is attached on the right to a brick section built in 1957 by C. R. Barnsley. The main material is concrete and represents the mid-twentieth century's interpretation of public architecture. The entrance rooms contain an Information and Help desk, the General Post Office and Warwick Library. Although it is attached to the Old Shire Hall, there is no public access through to Northgate Street. In the small water garden at the front of the building is sculpture that Warwick County Council commissioned to celebrate the millennium. It was designed and created by Rachel Higgins, a young Warwickshire sculptor. The theme of wildlife, three herons catching fish, offers a touch of the countryside in this busy market square.

New Shire Hall.

Market Hall Museum

The Market Hall is a good example of a public building of the late seventeenth century. It is built in local sandstone, with a large and overhanging roof. The arcades were originally open for market stalls and below ground floor level is a small lock-up used until 1848 for felons awaiting trial. This windowless cell serves to remind us of the tough treatment of those who brushed with the law. The elegance of the building was probably lost on them – impressed on their memories would be confinement and despair.

In 1836 the Warwickshire Natural History & Archaeological Society created a museum in this building and it was during the Victorian era that the arcades were enclosed. By 1932 the Society could not afford the upkeep and offered it to the County Council. Demolition was discussed but fortunately nothing happened until 1962, when it was restored, and it is now a very fine museum. Along with all the other exhibits, there is also a model of Warwick before the Great Fire. A well-stocked shop will encourage visitors to purchase reminders of their day in Warwick.

Market Hall Museum.

The Collegiate Church of St Mary

St Mary's church was founded by Roger de Beaumont, second Earl of Warwick, in 1123. It is called a collegiate church because he also established a college of canons, a community of ordained clergy who worked in the world rather than in monastic isolation. The only part of the original foundation that survives is a section of the Norman crypt.

Thomas Beauchamp, Earl of Warwick (*d.* 1369), began the rebuilding of the surviving choir in the fourteenth century and his tomb stands in front of the high altar. A more elaborate monument was planned by his grandson, Richard Beauchamp, Earl of Warwick, who commissioned the famous Beauchamp Chapel that lies to the south of the choir. Sadly the earl did not live to see his glorious chapel finished – work was completed twenty-three years after his death in 1439.

The destruction of St Mary's by the Great Fire was tragic as it could have been avoided. People whose homes were burning rushed into the church to seek refuge from the flames.

St Mary's Collegiate Church.

Unfortunately, they also brought in salvaged possessions that still contained smouldering embers. Wood and other inflammable materials in the church caught fire and this spread very fast, subsequently destroying most of the building, leaving only the fabric of the chancel and the Beauchamp Chapel. Firefighters managed to save the chapel – probably on the express orders of Lord Brooke, whose ancestors are so vividly displayed in this historic place of rest.

After the fire the great London architect Sir Christopher Wren was invited to prepare a design, which has survived. However, the plans of Sir William Wilson, a sculptor from Leicester, were accepted. He chose Warwick stone but it proved inadequate for the purpose; in 1700 cracks appeared and the tower had to be demolished to the level of the church roof. Again Sir Christopher Wren was approached, this time for advice, and he suggested that the tower should stand independently from the church and be built over the road. Francis Smith, the Warwick builder, and his brother William were given the commission to design and build the tower following Wren's advice. Rather than the softer Warwick stone, they used local hardwearing Shrewley stone. The west wall of the church was thickened to allow the tower to project over the roadway.

The new church was finished in 1704. It is a good example of eighteenth-century town church architecture, and a practical replacement for the fifteenth-century Perpendicular style. Francis Smith chose to reflect this medieval style by including elements such as niches on the tower and Perpendicular-style windows, but he increased their size. This makes the interior light and spacious. There is much to see, including the chapel of the Warwickshire Regiment with its evocative historical banners, several monuments to Warwick worthies and the Norman crypt. As well as the tomb of Richard Beauchamp, the Beauchamp Chapel also contains the tombs of Robert Dudley, Earl of Leicester, his

Drainpipe decoration.

The Nave.

son, the 'Noble Imp', and Dudley's brother Ambrose, Earl of Warwick. This chapel is a constant reminder of the Dudleys and their association with Warwick. The west window contains pieces of fifteenth-century stained glass. It was damaged during the Civil Wars but when the glass was reset, it was not to the original design.

The church has not been damaged since the Civil War. However, this gem in Warwick's crown recently received a forewarning of potential disaster and it came from a very significant source. A plaster angel on the ceiling near the altar detached itself and smashed to pieces on the floor below. Was this heroic act of self-destruction a message from on high that the fabric of the church was deteriorating and needed refurbishment? The angel's fall focused attention on other problems in the fabric and decoration and prompted St Mary's to plan a huge fundraising programme of £1.2 million.

St Mary's is a popular venue for concerts that help to fill the coffers. Visitors can also contribute by making purchases from the shop, climbing the steps to the tower and making generous donations to ensure that this ancient church will be conserved for many years to come.

The Beauchamp Chapel.

The College Garden

The old College of the Vicars Choral once occupied the site of this small, secluded garden to the north of St Mary's churchyard. The College had been founded by Earl Richard Beauchamp in the fifteenth century, and during that period housed a dean, six canons and two priests. It was a rich foundation, owning property within both the town and the nearby settlements of Longbridge and Heathcote. After the dissolution of the monasteries in 1544, the College and grounds were bought by the Wagstaffes of Tachbrook.

In 1699 Warwick Town Corporation, acting as trustees of the King Henry VIII Endowed Trust (set up to benefit the people of Warwick), bought the property for £260 to house the town's grammar school. Warwick School, as it became known, remained here until the school moved to new buildings along the Myton road in 1879. Warwick School is the oldest grammar school for boys in the country, and dates from the time of King Edward the Confessor, who reigned 1042–66. In 1880 it was recorded that Alderman Tibbits thought that the old buildings of the College ought to be preserved. However, his suggestion was not taken up and the property was sold to a London solicitor who demolished the building in 1882 and sold off the materials.

The original college building surrounded a courtyard and stood in its own grounds, probably with a herb garden for the medicinal needs of the inmates. On the 1851 Board of Health plan of Warwick the college is shown with an informal garden to the south-east, adjoining the wall of the 'tink-a-tank' path which leads from St Mary's churchyard to the road known as The Butts. The name 'tink-a-tank' derives from the sound of studded boots or wooden clogs – the usual footwear of previous times – on the hard surface of the path. The garden had trees, a lawn, and ornamental beds. The lawn was bisected by informal paths dividing the garden into separate areas. On the north-west side of the building there were further small gardens with planted beds. One small bed made in a right-angled shape with parallel lines drawn within it probably indicated a vegetable patch. A print of the College dated 1855 shows a typical Elizabethan or possibly Jacobean façade with gables, the lower windows being probably of a later date. The interior courtyard facades had attractive wooden carving. In another print of the same date, gardeners are shown tending the garden, which has ivy-covered walls, beds of shrubs and mature trees.

Today there is no trace left of the old college and garden as it used to be. The only visible evidence of the Vicars Choral College is the old stone garden walls. Set in part of the old wall to the north, just beyond the boundary of the present garden, there is a wide archway built in similar stone which was probably the original entrance to the college from The Butts. Today this archway just leads in to the modern vicarage, with its own garden. The boundary of St Mary's churchyard forms the garden wall to the south-west, and the south-eastern wall edges the 'tink-a-tank' walk from Church Street to The Butts. Leaving the churchyard, a gothic arched gateway offers

The College Garden.

an intriguing glimpse into the present simple garden. The wrought-iron gate opens down steps to a path of stone slabs leading across a large lawn and out to The Butts beyond. To the north of the lawn and along the 'tink-a-tank' wall, mature trees make the garden a pleasant sheltered retreat, with benches which are a favourite spot for a sunny lunchtime break. The pleached lime trees which run along the tink-a-tank walk were planted in 1742.

The College Garden, the entrance from St Mary's churchyard.

Lord Leycester Hotel

This elegant, apparently early nineteenth-century building has a fascinating history spanning many centuries and has evolved into a hotel which blends a strong sense of history with modern hospitality.

It was originally two house plots which were brought together as a single large house and then, in the early nineteenth century, converted back into two houses, known as 17 and 19 Jury Street. Number 19, the right hand part, was occupied by a glazier in the sixteenth century and, in the 1592 will of Nicholas Eyffler, was referred to as the 'new house', with a parlour, a glass chamber, and a barn, the surviving account book confirming the rebuilding. It then passed through various hands until being acquired by Thomas Archer in 1669.

Number 17, the left-hand part, is first referred to in 1575, when it was part of the 'manor' of Warwick, when it was held for annual rent by Julian Sheldon, widow of Robert. Sir Bartholomew Hales, knight, had acquired it by 1619 and, by his death in 1626, had 'erected and newe built' it. It was then sold to Thomas Wagstaffe and, in 1655, was granted to Mary Rous, wife of John Rous and widow of Thomas Wagstaffe, for life. By 1669 it was recorded by the son of the next owner, Thomas Ward, that his father, Rowley Ward, had 'not long since' built his house, although this must have been before 1662. In this year, 1669, this house was also sold to Thomas Archer. He then rebuilt both

Lord Leycester Hotel.

properties as a single, large, stone-built town house, the property remaining with the family until the end of the eighteenth century. During this century the property was let as the Three Tuns, the house having survived the great fire of 1694.

In about 1800 the property was sold and divided into two houses. The front courtyard of No. 17 was then filled in and both houses were re-fronted in brick, with the new owner of No. 17 also purchasing a small property adjoining, which was made into a coach house by 1804. By the mid-1800s 19 Jury Street was a girls' boarding house for Warwick High School. In 1880 John Allin Smith purchased 19 Jury Street from the Evans family. The property eventually passed to his wife, Charlotte Chapman Abbotts.

In 1925 Arthur Henry Tyack, the owner of The Warwick Arms Hotel, bought 19 Jury Street from Mrs Abbotts in order to develop the house into a top-class hotel for the town. It opened in 1926 as The Lord Leycester Hotel. The next year he purchased 17 Jury Street and, combining it with No. 19, reinstated the building as a single property. In the 1930s the hotel was extended, with additional bedrooms overlooking the church and lovely gardens, which were converted to the car park during the 1940s.

During the Second World War the hotel was requisitioned for use by the Ministry of Production. In 1943 the hotel was handed over to the US military, which built the 'tower' extension and used the property as an Officers' Club. At the end of the war the hotel was handed back to Mr Tyack. When he died in 1951 the property passed to his executors, who sold the building in 1963 to The Lord Leycester Hotel Limited.

They extended what was the restaurant at the back of the hotel to create the impressive Greville Suite, now the hotel's principal function room. In the 1980s the hotel was updated so that all bedrooms had en-suite facilities and new purpose-built meeting rooms were added. The present owners, MGM Hotels Limited, have just carried out another a major refurbishment which reflects the style and ambience of the twenty-first century without losing the old-fashioned charm.

Dining Room.

St John's House Museum

St John's House is the best-preserved Jacobean-style house in Warwick, built of stone, with a tiled roof, stone gables and mullioned windows. Although much altered inside and around the back, the front is a good example of the original architectural style. The present house sits on the site of a hospital dedicated to St John founded by the Earl of Warwick in the reign of Henry II (1154–89). Its purpose was to give lodging to travellers and to help the local poor and infirm. The charter of 1546 states that the hospital was founded to maintain a master or warden, two chaplains and two poor men, as well as dispensing hospitality. Very little is known about the buildings. John Speed's map of Warwick (1610) shows some surviving structures but this is about seventy years after the hospital ceased to function.

In 1540 St John's was granted by King Henry VIII to Anthony Stoughton, of Surrey, a servant of the Queen, for his lifetime. Anthony's great-nephew, another Anthony, inherited the site and began to redevelop it for his home. The rear part of the house was probably rebuilt in 1626 but it was not until 1660 that the frontage was complete. It was built in the Jacobean style of the 1660s, very similar to two other houses in Warwick, The Marble House, and Joyce Pool House. The builder has never been identified.

The house passed down through the Stoughton family until it was sold in 1798 to the Earl of Warwick and was then lived in by a series of tenants. For the next century the building housed schools, sometimes for young ladies and sometimes for young gentlemen. The first school was St John's Academy, a boys' boarding school under the headship of William Fowler. In 1828 the school was taken over by the Misses Fowler, relatives of the first headmaster, who turned it into a school for young ladies. However, by 1845 it became once again a Boarding Academy for Young Gentlemen with the Revd Townsend as headmaster. It was listed in 1880s as St John's Schools and by then it combined the education of older boys with a preparatory department, where the Misses Townsends received a limited number of little boys under twelve. Perhaps finding little boys too energetic, the ladies changed the school back to a girls' school. The fees were 30 guineas per annum, for which they received a tutoring in French, music, writing, arithmetic, geography, use of globes, Ancient and Modern History, with Plain and ornamental needlework. The school went bankrupt in 1900.

The Ladies' School took up the ground floor and the upper floors were let as apartments. They became very popular with artists, and an unofficial colony of artists evolved whose studios were open to the public. However, the lodgings, which could be reserved by travellers and visitors, were not perhaps up to the standards expected. Several clients described them as 'somewhat primitive' and one reported that she had looked out of her bedroom door in the morning and 'found a duck quacking at it, which had waddled up the great Jacobean staircase on the chance of getting a meal'. The lodgings for visitors and ducks did not continue. After Miss Townsend, the house was let to a series of tenants as a unit, complete with large reception rooms, many bedrooms, servants' accommodation and cottage.

Mr Ludlow took the tenancy in 1915 but he died within a few years. He was followed by Mr and Mrs Rice, a wealthy American couple, who lived at St John's between 1919 and 1922, after which they sought the sea air at Norfolk. Mrs Marsh then moved in but only stayed a year. However, during that time she had spent between £3,500 and £4,000 on work which included a tennis court and improvements to drains and plumbing.

In 1923 the house was advertised by Godfrey-Payton, Land Agents and Surveyors of Warwick. The house contained 'a large entrance hall, with a very fine old oak staircase, old oak panelled dining room, morning room/library, beautiful drawing room and oak panelled sitting room, six bed and dressing rooms and four other bedrooms, and two bathrooms. There was also an annexe containing two reception rooms, four bathrooms, with domestic offices. It was offered either unfurnished, (the lease having seven years to run) for £2,000, or unfurnished £500 per annum.' Among those who made enquiries were Anthony Eden MP, The King's School Warwick, and a prospective headmistress with plans to open a girls' school. Trust House Hotels expressed interest in turning the house into a select hotel …

for the more wealthy American, who would be very glad indeed to stay at such a place, and would not be careful as to the expense of doing so.

Eventually the War Department took the house and used it for the Infantry Record Office of the Home Counties and East Anglian Brigades. They vacated in 1958. The County

St John's House Museum.

Council and Royal Warwickshire Regiment asked the earl for the lease but in 1959 it was announced that Warwick Castle Estates were to be sold so the council decided to buy St John's. Field Marshal Montgomery strongly requested that the building should become a museum and after a great deal of financial negotiation, and with the help of £2,500 from the Regiment, it was purchased for £10,000. It was to be used as a county museum, with part of the building leased to The Royal Warwickshire Regiment.

Field Marshal Montgomery of Alamein opened St John's House Museum at 3 p.m. on Wednesday 2 August 1962. The ground floor was used for exhibitions and the Regimental Museum was placed on the first floor. Attics were used for storage. Sixty years later, the museum is a popular place to visit, especially for families and schools. Schoolchildren were invited to visit the schoolroom and re-enact a typical lesson. It became obvious that hands-on history was exciting and an excellent way to offer an out-of-school experience in the environment of a museum. Over the entrance is the word EDUCATION – painted on when the building was in use as a school. Although hardly discernible now, it is a reminder that learning in this building has a long history, now proudly continued by the Council's Heritage Education Service.

St John's House Museum detail.

The Garden of St John's House

The imposing mansion of St John's House, located by the traffic lights at the bottom of Smith Street, is home to part of the County Museum, and also to the Museum of the Royal Warwickshire Regiment. Although much of the original garden has subsequently been built on, the monumental gates and the wide approach to the main door still remain. There is a fine old sandstone wall surrounding the present garden, which is laid mainly to lawn but also has some mature trees, and a colourful border along the west wall. There are two old and attractive statues of a shepherd and shepherdess in this border. To the south of this garden, old yew hedges surround a space originally laid out as a bowling green, a fashionable feature in gentlemen's gardens in the seventeenth and eighteenth centuries. Beyond this area there is an attractive walkway with modern wood carvings which leads to the large public park of St Nicholas, with its ornamental gardens, playing fields, and walks adjacent to the River Avon.

St John's House, old statues of a shepherd and shepherdess in the garden.

St Nicholas Park

The Common to the west of the town has always been the main area available to the people of Warwick for public recreation. Several annual fairs used to take place here, providing popular diversions and fun for working folk. The fairs included the May Fair, the Cherry Wakes, the Meadow Wake, and, held in September in the centre of town, the Mop. The Mop was the annual hiring fair, held in many other towns as well, where those seeking employment of all kinds for the following year came with a sign of their trade. Housemaids carried a mop, hence the name of the fair. Nowadays the only remaining part of the Mop is the funfair which was always associated with it, and the day when the funfair fills the old market square is eagerly awaited by the young folk of the town.

In the eighteenth century bowls was a popular pastime, and there were at least four bowling greens in the town, two of which are commemorated in local street or pub names. In Victorian times Warwick was comparatively slow to develop a designated park for public recreation. Nearby Leamington Spa had its first public park in 1862, but it was the end of the nineteenth century before there was a move to create a public park in Warwick, and 1928 before the council acquired the whole of St Nicholas' meadow for this purpose. The meadow was the area bounded by the churchyard of St Nicholas and the land belonging to St John's to the north, and the river to the south. Traditionally there were common grazing rights on the meadow, and the occasional remnants of the old 'ridge and furrow' ploughing system once established on medieval arable land all over the Midlands provide evidence of ancient arable cultivation here. In 1773 the meadow was enclosed, largely absorbing the common grazing rights. In 1793 the new bridge and approach road to Warwick were completed. The approach road forms the western boundary to the park, and the Earl of Warwick had wanted an oak fence, trees and a hawthorn hedge along this road to preserve the rural approach to the town, but this was never fully implemented.

During the late 1920s the area of the new park was gradually raised to alleviate flooding. This was carried out by dumping the town's rubbish over the area, and covering it with earth when the desired levels had been attained. In 1930 the Borough Surveyor drew up a design for the whole park, which included ornamental gardens with trees, shrubs and flower beds, a children's play area, tennis courts and a bowling green, a riverside walk and a large open grassed area. Soon after this date the central lime walk leading from the gates for the entrance from the Banbury Road through the gardens was planted. At the same time the brook running through the site was canalised and the edges set with low ornamental plants. During the 1930s various amenities were put in place, including a children's play area, two hard tennis courts, a golf putting green, a tea pavilion and an ornamental garden shelter thatched with Norfolk reed.

In 1933 the Earl of Warwick donated a fine pair of ornamental wrought iron entrance gates from the Banbury road. These were made by the local blacksmith at Emscote, near St John's. The Earl specified that the new entrance was not to be used by motor vehicles! As a result, vehicular access has always been along the road adjacent to the churchyard,

St Nicholas Park, in the gardens.

St Nicholas Park, in the gardens.

leading to the car park, which has now replaced the council's old horticultural nursery. In 1935 a new entrance to the park from the north-east was laid out as a walk, bordered by trees and mown grass, from the Emscote Road beyond St John's. The land was bought from the Earl of Warwick.

In 1936 the bank of the river was strengthened with a sloping concrete wall, and a grass path was laid along the bank. Willows were planted on the river side, and laburnums and hawthorns along the inside or park side of the path. In 1938–39 the area of land known as Myton Fields, between the Myton Road and Warwick School to the south, and the river to the north, was bought from the Earl of Warwick. The Earl reduced the price by £1,500 as a gift to the town. The area is now very popular, particularly on weekends and Bank Holidays, when people like to park their cars on the grass and enjoy a picnic by the river.

The Development of Sports Facilities in the Park

From at least the 1850s boys had enjoyed bathing in the river, using an inlet with a little beach just east of the new bridge. Known as the Scour, this bathing place became increasingly popular for nude bathing by men as well as boys. This spectacle shocked the sensibilities of the Victorian ladies taking boating trips downriver from the Emscote Bridge tearooms towards Warwick Castle, so in 1873 the first public bathing pool was made at the Scour. The flow of the river itself was utilised to make the pool, which was screened with planting, and swimming was restricted to men and boys. Warwick was one of the first towns to make use of the Avon to provide a bathing area. Worcester, Leamington Spa and also Stratford-on-Avon all developed river bathing places. At Warwick there were problems from the start with the purity of the water because of the effluents discharged upstream from Coventry and Leamington. The water intake was filtered from 1929, when mixed bathing was also introduced. Eventually, increasing maintenance problems together with health concerns following the polio epidemics of 1947 and 1955 led to the enforced closure of this pool in 1955. By 1960 a new open-air pool had been built close to the ornamental gardens, and this was in turn superceded in 1983 by a modern indoor pool.

Boating had always taken place on the river, and by 1934 there was a boathouse at the Scour. This was taken over by the local sailing club. In the 1960s both the Sea Scouts and the Sea Cadets were using a base on the river. In 1997 the Sailing Club was disbanded, though individually owned sailboats are still used on the river and kept on the south bank at Myton Fields. Rowing boats and motor boats are available for hire from the boathouse by Castle Bridge.

In 1938 the local fishing club requested the sole right to fish the Avon from the park, but the Council refused, allowing fishing to be freely available to the public in the park. Fishing clubs have leased the right to fish from the south side of the river, at Myton Fields, since 1945. In 1945–47 a string of pools was created at the east end of the park to provide fishing for young people and the disabled. This area has also become an interesting habitat for wildlife, and for native water-loving plants such as the yellow flag iris and purple loosestrife.

The implementation of the ideas for sports pitches contained in the 1930 plan for the park was sporadic due to the Depression, and to the subsequent lack of available funds. The ground where the levels were being raised was not properly seeded and finished until after the 1940–45 war. Over the years the sports pitches made on this reconditioned land began to show signs of uneven settlement, and the demand for playing fields in the park diminished as clubs found pitches elsewhere. Recreational requirements changed over time, and the local authority has provided new facilities to meet this need. In 1984 a BMX track was made for young cyclists, in 1989 an all-weather sports pitch with flood lighting was installed, in 1998 a skateboard ramp was built to cater for this new craze and in 2000 a basketball pitch was laid out.

Today St Nicholas Park is a large, open grass area catering for a wide range of recreational needs. Adjacent to the main entrance from the Banbury road there is an attractive garden of lawns and flower beds crossed by avenues of ornamental trees. There is mini golf, a paddling pool and a children's playground nearby, and a pleasant pavilion supplies light meals and teas. Beyond there is the swimming pool, the all-weather pitch and other pitches, and a large open area of turf used for informal recreation. The riverside walk provides a pleasant place to wander, leading at the eastern end of the park to the new fishing pools area. From here it is possible to continue along a path which runs beside the river right to Leamington Spa.

St Nicholas Park, the River Avon and Myton Fields with the bridge in the background.

Above: St Nicholas Park, one of the landscaped pools, with purple loosestrife and reedmace, and a heron on the far bank.

Right: St Nicholas Park, the Charter Bridge plaque, with Warwick Castle in the distance seen across the Park. This modern bridge, for cyclists and pedestrians, crosses the Avon from the Myton Road to the Park.

The Mill Garden

The Mill Garden, the garden of No. 55 Mill Street, lies right at the end of Mill Street, which leads from the eighteenth-century castle entrance opposite St Nicholas' church down to the River Avon. The far end of the garden is adjacent to the old castle mill from which the street gets its name. The garden has a magical setting at the foot of the castle façade, with the river running by and Caesar's tower overlooking the scene. From the lawn running down to the river can be seen the ruins of the old, narrow fourteenth-century bridge. This was once the only bridge over the river for several miles each way, but by the eighteenth century traffic was very heavy and the bridge itself had become unsafe. The Earl of Warwick decided to build the present bridge upstream, moving the road to connect with it. Following the partial collapse of the old bridge in a flood, the Earl dismantled it sufficiently to make it unusable as a bridge, leaving it as a fine romantic ruin. The site of the present Mill garden then became disused until 1902, when it first began to be cultivated as a tenanted garden.

In 1951 Arthur Measures and his family came to live at No. 55, and Mr Measures created the present garden over the following sixty years or so. Mr Measures' own

The Mill Garden, borders of flowers with the cottage in the background.

description, printed in 1998 in his guide to the garden, gives his vision of what he wished to create:

> I wanted to take advantage of the wonderful views, if possible one at a time. I wanted a garden in which besides cultivated plants some wild things thrived, both flowers and creatures. Beside swans on the millpond … and the sound of water falling over the weirs, I wanted birdsong and the flitter of butterflies, whilst the garden was to remain a cottage garden … Above all, the garden was to be a place of peace and beauty.

Following the purchase of some adjoining land running right up to the castle walls, Mr Measures was able to start turning his dream into reality. The garden, though not large, is famed for the quality of its planting, which is in a predominantly cottage garden style and provides year-round colour. Winding paths where flowering plants spill out over the edges lead down from the cottage to the river, with the backdrop of the old ruined bridge arches. A path continues along the river bank, through a garden arch carrying a profusion of clematis and roses, to a small lawn which opens out to views of the borders right under the castle walls.

On the left the garden ends along the bank of the river, which winds south over the weir and in front of the castle. At the far end of the lawn the garden vista is closed by stands of dramatic bog plants such as *Rheum* and *Gunnera*. Ron Sidwell, in his book on West Midland gardens, commented on the garden's great variety and beauty, and said that he could not recall seeing *Gunnera manicata* quite so fine anywhere. To the right there are

Above left: The Mill Garden, the remains of the old ruined bridge seen from the garden.

Above right: The Mill Garden, hydrangeas by one of the paths.

beds of herbaceous plants backed by interesting shrubs, and a path leads to a small area where plants such as hydrangea in variety and the unusual *Veratrum nigrum* enjoy the shadier conditions. Here the old toll stocks can be seen, still remaining in their original place and now designated a 'listed building'.

A small vegetable garden for the house and a nursery patch where plants are grown on for sale completes the tour of the garden. Immediately outside the garden itself, the great wall of the castle grounds has also been used as a backdrop for plants. These include climbing roses and clematis in variety, *Solanum jasminoides album*, and herbaceous plants with bold foliage such as *Onopordon*, the giant Scotch thistle, and the globe artichoke.

Over the years the garden has been open regularly, the entrance money being collected for charities to which many thousands of pounds have been given. Mr Measures always wanted to ensure that the garden continued to be maintained and open for visitors 'as a peaceful place for those in need of spiritual refreshment'. He would indeed be happy to know that since his death the cottage has been taken over and the garden lovingly maintained and kept open for the public by Julia, Mr Measures' daughter, and her husband David Russell.

The Mill Garden, the old stocks.

Warwick Castle

Warwick town and its castle are linked in people's minds as a perfect foil for each other. The castle is world-famous, visited by hundreds of thousands of people each year, and is considered by some to be the most visually stunning castle in England. From the imposing towers there are commanding views over the beautiful wooded countryside of Warwickshire. It is also fortunate that it has survived virtually undamaged by sieges or battles, and until 1978 was inhabited continuously by the earls of Warwick.

The foundation goes back to AD 917 when Ethelfleda, a Saxon princess, established a settlement on the hill. In 1068 William the Conqueror established a motte and bailey castle as part of a plan to safeguard the Midlands before advancing against the northern rebels. Henry de Beaumont, younger son of a powerful Norman family, was given the responsibility of castellan or constable and in 1088 William II rewarded Henry's loyalty by creating him Earl of Warwick.

It was an excellent site for a castle as it stood on a sandstone bluff and the river had cut away the rock from a cliff, providing a natural defence. By the fourteenth century the castle was developed and rebuilt in stone. A gatehouse tower and barbican were connected by high curtain walls to two great angle towers, Caesar's Tower on the south side and Guy's Tower on the north. A dry moat protected the entrance drawbridge.

Many dramatic events are woven into the castle's past. In 1312, Piers Gaveston, the unpopular favourite of Edward II, was captured by Guy de Beauchamp, Earl of Warwick, and imprisoned in Warwick Castle until his execution on 9 June 1312. During the Wars of the Roses in the fifteenth century Richard Neville, Earl of Warwick, imprisoned Edward IV in the castle dungeons. No wonder he became known to history as 'the kingmaker'!

The Dudley family was also closely connected with the castle. John Dudley, who was created Earl of Warwick in 1547 and Duke of Northumberland in 1551, attempted to make his daughter-in-law, Lady Jane Grey, queen after the death of Edward VI. He was imprisoned in the Tower of London with his five sons, convicted of high treason and executed. His eldest surviving son, Ambrose, although imprisoned with his father, was later reprieved and became the second Earl of Warwick of the second creation in 1561. Elizabeth granted the castle to him in 1562. His younger brother, Robert Dudley, the favourite of Elizabeth I, arranged a Royal Progress in 1572 and she stayed at the castle for several nights in August. During her visit she also travelled the 'fairest way' to Robert Dudley's home, Kenilworth Castle. Warwick's castle was obviously not large enough to accommodate Elizabeth and her retinue – she did not travel light! A timber building was erected specially for her comfort, and her host, Ambrose Dudley, was obliged to move to the Priory.

Elizabeth loved to be entertained and during the stay a mock battle was staged in the grounds. Two 'forts' were constructed and a dozen cannons and a dozen mortars were fired. Added to this spectacle were fireworks, one of which was a flying 'dragon' which cast out huge flames and squibs. This landed on the fort. What happened next was one

Above: Warwick Castle.

Left: River Road Gate.

of the worst nightmares of townspeople in the centuries when houses were mostly timber and thatch. One ball of fire landed on a house at the end of the bridge and it went up in flames. Oblivious to the cannons, mortars and all other noises, the owner and his wife were in bed asleep. Fortunately they were rescued but lost everything they owned. Four other houses were damaged. Elizabeth asked to see the couple and gave them £25 12s 8d towards their losses. This money had been contributed by her and her courtiers. The owners of four other houses that suffered damage from the entertainment were not so fortunate.

After these exciting times the castle then gradually fell into a parlous state of repair, with parts of the windows, walls and towers having fallen down. The stewardship passed to Sir Fulke Greville in 1604. Later, Sir William Dugdale, the Warwickshire antiquarian, reported that Greville had spent more than £20,000 in repairing and adorning it, making it 'a place not only of great strength but extraordinary delight, with most pleasant gardens, walls and thickets, such as in this part of England can hard parallel'.

Green Drawing Room.

The Civil Wars of the 1640s augured dangerous times so the castle was put in a state of defence. In the absence of Lord Brooke, Sir Edward Peyto of Chesterton, with a Parliamentary garrison, was besieged at the castle by the Earl of Northampton, the Royalist Lord Lieutenant of the county. During an exchange of fire several besiegers were killed. Prisoners taken after the battle of Edge Hill were confined in Caesar's and Guy's towers. Later, the towers provided a storage space for goods plundered from the Royalists after the Battle of Worcester. A governor was appointed in 1643 and a garrison was maintained there until 1660, when Colonel Hawksworth was ordered to disband the garrison and deliver possession of the castle to Lord Brooke.

Repairs to the castle had been carried out during the Interregnum (1649–69) but on regaining possession, Lord Brooke started to provide new outbuildings and remodel the principal rooms on the lines of the great houses of the day. Rebuilding continued throughout his lifetime and through that of his successor. When Francis Greville, the eighth Baron Brooke, later the first Earl of Warwick of the third creation, came of age in 1740, he began a period of major improvements to the castle and its surroundings, including the demolition of houses in Castle Street to accommodate stables. George Greville succeeded his father in 1773 and put the finishing touches to alterations of the rooms.

The earl also made great alterations to part of the town as he wanted to create a new bridge over the Avon upstream from the old one, to provide a new approach to the town, the Banbury Road. The old bridge was in a state of decay but instead of replacing it *in situ*, it suited the earl's purpose to take more land into the castle grounds and create a distance between him and the inhabitants, as he considered the town was 'enough to debauch anybody that is not already steady and sober'. This huge disruption had major effects on the town, requiring several streets to be demolished. He also extended the castle grounds so that people were prevented from passing too close to his main entrance. The cost of the building was £3,258, exclusive of the approach roads, and the bridge was to be maintained by the earl for seven years, after which the burden would fall upon the King Henry VIII Endowed Trust, whose foundation rests on the 1545 charter of Henry VIII to the town of Warwick.

By 1802 the estate as a whole was approaching a financial crisis and in the ensuing crash the earl found himself in the position of a bankrupt. Estates were sold, workmen laid off and any further improvement ceased. It was time for financial retrenchment and with the exception of work to the foundation of Caesar's Tower there is no evidence of any extensions carried out on the castle or grounds. Internal improvements that were carried out were much more modest. However, by the 1850s the family fortunes had been reversed and Anthony Salvin, the famous nineteenth-century architect and restorer of castles, was employed to restore the Watergate Tower and carry out alterations to the river front of the domestic range. Queen Victoria visited the fourth earl in 1858. He was no doubt grateful that she, unlike her royal ancestor, would not expect him to bankrupt himself on her behalf.

Sadly, a fire in 1871 caused considerable damage, the most serious loss being the Great Hall. The restoration was aided by public subscription, which commenced in 1872 and ultimately reached £9,651. Other apartments untouched by the fire remained unaltered and the work was complete by 1875.

Above: Great Hall.

Right: Sixteenth-century armour for a knight and horse.

Individual tourists had been visiting the castle since the end of the seventeenth century, and by the nineteenth century the numbers has increased dramatically. However, by 1885 it would appear that the visiting public was becoming a nuisance as the earl closed the castle to them, causing consternation in the town. A local report stated, 'One day last week eight American visitors who were staying at one of the principal hotels left somewhat hurriedly in consequence of their being unable to gain admission to the castle.' However, it soon opened again and by 1900 had a ticket office and was employing a permanent guide.

The castle enjoyed a renaissance during the life of the fifth earl, Francis, and his wife Daisy. House parties, garden parties and long weekends were the order of the day. Daisy became a great socialite and she and the earl became part of the Marlborough House set whose head was Edward, Prince of Wales. The countess became his mistress so Edward and his friends became frequent visitors to the castle. One of those weekends

Guy's Tower and Ballista.

in 1898 is vividly displayed today as a tableau for visitors to recapture those halcyon days.

By 1936 Arthur Mee was enthusing not just that 'these walls have seen something of the splendour of every generation of our [English] story', with rooms 'rich in treasure beyond the dreams of avarice', but also that 'their rooms are open to all who will'.

Throughout the twentieth century successive earls expanded the castle's tourism potential until, in 1978, after 374 years in the Greville family, Lord Brooke sold his family home to Madame Toussaud's. It became one of the most popular venues in Great Britain for entertainment and leisure. During the last thirty years millions of visitors have revelled in the exploration of the many rooms of the castle. Many have experienced the thrill of fear when visiting dark dungeons, and 'haunted' rooms, which was only too real to prisoners of previous centuries. Today a visit to Warwick Castle is enjoyable and safe!

Castle Mill and Weir.

Warwick Castle Gardens

Warwick Castle, one of the most important defensive sites in the kingdom, has had gardens since at least medieval times. The earliest recorded reference to a garden is in a survey carried out in 1576, four years after Queen Elizabeth I's visit to the castle as the guest of Ambrose Dudley, Earl of Warwick. The survey refers to the Queen's gardens 'next Avon without the Castle walls'. Ambrose was brother to Robert Dudley, Earl of Leicester, who created the formal gardens at Kenilworth Castle for the Queen on her visit in 1575. The gardens at Warwick were likely to have been laid out to a similar formal plan. Sir Fulke, later Baron Greville (1554–1628), spent more than £20,000, then an enormous sum, on the restoration of the castle and its grounds. The grounds included Ethelfleda's Mount, built against the western castle walls.

In 1678 Thomas Baskerville, a visitor to the town, related that the walls of the castle encompassed a 'pale and dainty bowling green, set about with laurel, firs and other curious (interesting) trees'. This courtyard area had previously been used for the stables and outhouses. Although the bowling green has long gone, the courtyard still retains its plain grass centre, which enhances the grandeur of the surrounding castle walls and

Warwick Castle, Ethelfleda's Mound.

Warwick Castle, view across the gardens and Castle Park from Ethelfleda's Mound.

Warwick Castle, mature cedars dating from the period of Capability Brown's work.

towers. A map prepared in 1711 by the cartographer James Fish and Charles Bridgeman, later the Royal Gardener, and held in the County Record Office shows two enclosed formal gardens adjacent to the castle. These reflect the popularity at the time of formal gardens after the Dutch style, following the gardening interests of Dutch King William III, who came to the throne in 1688 with his English wife Mary. William and Mary created the fine baroque gardens at Hampton Court Palace which have recently been fully restored.

During the peaceful (at least on English soil) and prosperous times of the first part of the eighteenth century, the gardens at the castle were completely altered and developed by Francis Greville, Lord Brooke (1727–73), who was later granted the title of Earl of Warwick. In the 1730s and 1740s the new movement towards an informal approach to landscaping grounds was becoming fashionable. Trend-setters in landscape gardening such as Lord Cobham of Stowe, in Buckinghamshire, George Lyttleton at Hagley, near Birmingham, and Sanderson Miller of Radway in south Warwickshire, the latter a designer of landscapes and mock ruined castles, were all part of Lord Brooke's social circle. Lord Brooke, however, had a problem; the town of Warwick came almost to the castle gates and grounds, exactly where he wanted to create his new gardens. So in 1744 he petitioned the Warwickshire Quarter Sessions to close a road leading down to the river from the north-west. He then began to demolish those houses between this road and the castle.

At this point Lord Brooke commissioned the help of Lancelot Brown, later better known as Capability Brown. Brown was then still in the employ of Lord Cobham, who allowed Brown to carry out work for a few of his friends. At Warwick Brown took away the formal gardens outside the Castle walls, replacing them with a sweeping grassed slope running down to the river. This area, still recognisable today, was carefully altered by earth modelling, and planted with many new specimen trees. Some of these trees, in particular some cedars of Lebanon, have now reached a magnificent maturity. Brown's work also included setting a new circular carriage drive within the grassed courtyard, and landscaping the old Castle Park beyond the river.

In the park, a new boundary belt was planted as well as several new clumps of trees. A new coach drive was laid out around the park to take Lord Brooke's visitors to see the improvements. The drive led over a small hill known as Temple Hill, from which there was a fine view. The name refers back to the Knights Templar who had originally held a manor within the park. At the southern end of the park the rising ground was planted with trees, and the Ram Brook, which flows into the Avon here, was dammed to form a new canal-like pool. On this higher ground a hunting lodge known as Spiers Lodge was built, commanding a fine view back towards the castle itself, a view commemorated in a drawing by Paul Sandby which is now held in the Warwickshire County Record Office. In early spring, the woods in this area are full of fine drifts of snowdrops. Brown's first payment from Lord Brooke was in 1749, and he continued to work at Warwick long after he had set up as a private consultant in 1751.

Horace Walpole, that indefatigable commentator on this period, wrote after a visit in 1751 that the castle was enchanting, and that little Brooke (he was short in stature even for the eighteenth century), 'who would have chuckled to have been born in an age of clipped hedges and cockle shell avenues, has submitted to let his park and garden be natural.'

Warwick Castle, the conservatory.

Warwick Castle, view through the Peacock Garden towards Pageant Field.

In 1773 George Greville succeeded to the earldom. In 1788 he petitioned for an Act of Parliament to build a new road bridge over the Avon upstream from the castle, as the old medieval bridge was in a poor state of repair. The great span of the new bridge was completed in 1793. The Earl then constructed a link road from this bridge into the town, creating at the same time a new entrance to the castle itself at the top of Mill Street. Completed in 1797, this driveway cut directly through the rock and indeed some of the cellars of the former houses on the site, making a shady and mysterious approach, with ferns growing out of the damp walls. At the far end, the visitor comes out into the sunlight where the dramatic outline of the castle is revealed on the skyline. This new approach embodied the ideals of the Picturesque Movement of the second half of the eighteenth century, using variety and introducing mystery and the element of surprise when suddenly coming upon a previously hidden vista.

In the 1770s the Earl came to own a great marble vase, the fragments of which had been recently excavated from the bed of a lake at Hadrian's Villa at Tivoli in Italy and reconstructed by Sir William Hamilton, British Envoy to Naples. Known as the Warwick Vase, it was housed in a special greenhouse designed by a local mason, William Eboral, and located in the area called Pageant Field. The Earl's brother, Charles Greville, who had been instrumental in the arrival of the Vase at Warwick, was a well-known horticulturalist and plant collector. In 1809 the Australian genus *Grevillea* was named after him, and the greenhouse today includes a representative collection of *Grevilleas*.

In the early Victorian period little was done in the gardens. The second earl had left the estate impoverished, and sales of other properties were necessary to keep the castle and its grounds afloat financially. In the early 1830s twin icehouses were constructed near what is now the Rose Garden. Before the days of refrigeration, the collection of ice during the winter was important, for it was used in the summer for cooling wine and food and for the production of ice cream.

In 1858 Queen Victoria and Prince Albert visited the castle and each planted a commemorative tree, an English oak and a Wellingtonia, *Sequoiadendron giganteum*, a native of California. Both trees flourished. New introductions of plants from abroad and the craze for bedding out plants for the summer led the fourth earl in 1868 to call in the designer Robert Marnock. Marnock produced plans for what is now the Peacock Garden, in front of the present Conservatory, and also for a new ornamental rose garden. The latter had decorative ironwork arches up which were grown climbing and rambling roses, and rose beds enclosed by dwarf box. After the First World War, and with the growing popularity of lawn tennis, a game which had been pioneered in Leamington Spa, part of this garden was demolished to make way for a tennis court.

In 1893 the fifth earl succeeded to the title. His wife, Francis Evelyn Maynard, always known as Daisy, had a large fortune and together the pair led a dazzling social life. A great deal of money was spent on improvements to the castle and its grounds. In 1894 a water-driven electric generating plant was installed in the mill house. This not only supplied the power for lighting in the castle, but also provided power for the electric launch used for river parties. The launch was housed in a new thatched boathouse on the river island. Lady Warwick had the island landscaped as part of the ornamental grounds, and she also collected a menagerie of animals which were kept on the island.

In 1900 a rock garden and small cascade were built alongside the Rose Garden; the plan for this still survives. At the same time Lady Warwick had alterations made to the greenhouse where the Warwick Vase was kept. The greenhouse, now to be called the Conservatory, had a new glass roof installed, together with a heating system and raised beds for the growing of ornamental plants, including, of course, *Grevilleas*. Lady Warwick also took an interest in Spiers Lodge, the hunting lodge situated on a bluff to the south of Castle Park, overlooking the river. She delighted in 'hideaways' of this nature, and had the Lodge enlarged, with steps down to the river. She also employed the landscape architect Harold Peto to design the small garden, which included formal topiary. In 1988 the local landscape architect Paul Edwards recreated the pergola garden at the Lodge.

Following the First World War it was found necessary to let the castle out for a short period to make ends meet. Eventually, in 1978 the family had to sell the castle and its contents to the Tussaud Group. Much restoration work was required, and under the expert guidance of Paul Edwards a programme of restoration was begun. A new entrance was constructed through the old stables for visitors, and a new car park was made. Unwanted scrub was cleared, and a programme of pruning and caring for the trees was undertaken. In 1985 Ethelfleda's Mound was again opened to the public, who can today enjoy the extensive views of the grounds, the river and the park from its summit. Research by Mr Edwards in the County Record Office revealed drawings both of the Peacock Garden in front of the Conservatory, and also of the old Rose Garden. These were the original drawings by Robert Marnock, dating from the mid-nineteenth century. They provided the pattern for the reinstatement of these gardens, in particular of the Rose Garden, the outlines of which had all but disappeared. Between 1983 and 1984 the latter was recreated on its old site, with newly replaced soil to avoid rose replant sickness in the soil where roses had previously been grown, and with new ornamental ironwork.

A mix of old roses, such as 'The Garland', a favourite of the designer Gertrude Jekyll, *Alberic Barbier*, and modern perpetual flowering roses bred by David Austin were planted. The overgrown rock garden and cascade were discovered to the north of the garden, and restored, and the old icehouses were made safe to be opened to the public. Previously there had been only one small gateway into the garden, for access by the family. New ironwork entrance gates more suitable for public access were made by local blacksmith George Worrall. The restored Rose Garden was opened by Diana, Princess of Wales, in 1986 and the restored Conservatory by Princess Margaret in 1989. Today there is again access to the river island below the castle, and a woodland garden has been established to the south of the Peacock Garden and Pageant Field.

The Merlin Entertainments Group, a worldwide organisation, has now taken over the running of Warwick Castle. Regular events such as outdoor concerts, also jousting and many other mock medieval displays are held in the grounds. The extensive gardens and Capability Brown's fine trees on the lawns running down to the river complete a superb setting for the old Castle itself. Compared to the fate which befell Kenilworth Castle, the town of Warwick is indeed fortunate to have such a historic castle with its magnificent grounds.

Warwick Castle, topiary peacock.

Warwick Castle, seen downriver from the bridge.

Acknowledgements

My thanks to Mark Booth, Stephen Wallsgrove and Gillian White for their support and encouragement. My special thanks are to my husband, Dick Cluley, for his photography, and for living with yet another book on Warwick with consummate patience.

Christine Cluley

I would like to thank Frances and Keith Smith of Warwick Books for the initial idea for this book, and for their subsequent encouragement in its production. My thanks are due to Richard Chamberlaine-Brothers and Christine Hodgetts, who have generously allowed the use of their unpublished research material. My thanks are due to Susan Rhodes and Geoffrey Smith, who have provided assistance in the preparation of the text, and also to the Master and the Brethren of the Lord Leycester Hospital, and Julia Russell of the Mill Garden for help and advice. I am also very grateful for the technical help and proof reading assistance given me by members of my family, without which the book would not have been completed.

Jennifer Meir

We would both like to thank Nicola Gale of Amberley Publishing who has been helpful throughout.

We are grateful to the following people who have been generous with their time and knowledge:

The staff of the Warwickshire County Record Office
Chris Begg
Edward Creasy
Alan Farrell
John Findley
Johanna Hobbs
Tim Harrison Jones
The Master and Brethren of the Lord Leycester Hospital
Derek Maudlin
Trudy Offer
Steve Smith
Neal Teago
Huw Williams
The Guides at St Mary's Collegiate Church

Picture Acknowledgements

Photography
Dick Cluley – Buildings
Jennifer Meir – Gardens
David Pratt – Warwick Racecourse
Warwick Racecourse Management – The common, the racecourse and the town

Map
Dick Cluley

Warwickshire County Record Office References
Warwickshire County Record Office standing on the site of Warwick Priory
CRO.CR1308 The Priory – Demolition, 1925
CRO.PV.WAR.pri1 p169 The Priory 1800
Browne, Joan D., Wallis, Shirley, Wallsgrove, Steven, *The Past In Warwick, A Family and a House*, ed. N. Alcock, Warwick University, 1992
Chamberlaine-Brothers, Richard, *Notes on the College* (Unpublished) W.C.R.O. Z502(sm)

Permission to Photograph Interiors of Buildings:
The Town Clerk, The Court House
The Proprietor, Oken's House
The Warden, Friends Meeting House
The Master, Lord Leycester Hospital
The Chairman, Hill Close Gardens
The Manager, Warwickshire County Record Office
Warwickshire County Council, The Old Shire Hall
St Mary's Collegiate Church
The Lord Leycester Hotel
The Manager, Warwick Castle

Further Reading

Bealby-Wright, Edmund, *Warwick, Birmingham*, Sketchbook Guides, 1994

Buttery, David, *Canaletto and Warwick Castle*, Phillimore, 1992

Cluley, Christine M., *Northgate Street*, Warwickshire County Council, 2005

Cluley, Christine M., *Warwick – A Short History and Guide*, Amberley, 2011

Farr, Michael, *The Great Fire of Warwick*, Dugdale Society, Hertford, Stephen Austin & Sons, 1992

Gomme, Andor, *Smith of Warwick, Francis Smith, Architect and Master-Builder*, Stamford, Shaun Tyas, 2000

Hill Close Gardens – Guide Book

Lines, Charles, *The Book of Warwick*, Barracuda Books, 1985

Meir, Jennifer, *Sanderson Miller and his Landscapes*, Phillimore, 2006

Morriss, Richard K., and Hoverd, K., *The Buildings of Warwick*, Stroud, Alan Sutton Publishing, 1994

Mowl, Tim, and James, Diane, *Historic Gardens of Warwickshire*, Redcliffe, 2011

Sidwell, Ron, *West Midland Gardens*, Alan Sutton Publishing, 1981

Tolkien, J. R. R., 'Kortirion Among the Trees'

Turpin, Jack, and Fox, W. Terry, *Battling Jack*, Mainstream Publishing Company (Edinburgh) Limited, 2005

Watkin, J. R., *Lord Leicester's Warwickshire*, Warwick District Council, 2011

Victoria County History, Vol. VIII

A restored summerhouse at Hill Close Gardens.

Contact Details

Buildings

These buildings have their own guidebooks and guides. These can be obtained from Tourist Information Office in the Court House.

THE COURT HOUSE
Jury Street
Tel. 01926 492212

Tourist Information
Tel. 01926 492212
www.visitwarwick.co.uk

WARWICKSHIRE YEOMANRY
MUSEUM
NB this museum is closed until 2013
Admission free

OKEN'S HOUSE
20 Castle Street
CV34 4BP
Tel. 01926 499307

THE FRIENDS MEETING HOUSE
39 High Street
enquiries@warwickquakers.org.uk
Tel. 01926 497732

LORD LEYCESTER HOSPITAL
High Street
Tel. 01926 491442
www.lordleycester.co.uk

The Queen's Own Hussars Museum is situated in the hospital.
Admission charge

WARWICKSHIRE COUNTY RECORD
OFFICE
Priory Park
Cape Road
CV34 4JS
Tel. 01926 738959
Email: recordoffice@warwickshire.gov.uk
www.warwickshire.gov.uk/
countyrecordoffice

THE OLD SHIRE HALL
Northgate Street
Tel. 01926 450000

COLLEGIATE CHURCH OF ST MARY
Old Square
Tel. 01926 400771
www.stmaryswarwick.org.uk
Admission – free but voluntary contributions are welcome.
Tower – admission charge.

Museums

COUNTY MUSEUM – MARKET HALL
Market Place
Tel. 01926 412500 or 412501
www.warwickshire.gov.uk
Admission Free

THE QUEEN'S OWN HUSSARS MUSEUM
(See entry for Lord Leycester Hospital)

ST JOHN'S HOUSE MUSEUM
Coten End

St John's Museum (Warwickshire
Museums)
Tel. 01926 412132
www.warwickshire.gov.uk

Royal Regiment of Fusiliers Museum
(Royal Warwickshire)
Tel. 01926 491653
www.warwickfusiliers.com
Admission Free

WARWICK CASTLE
Tel. 0870 442 2000
www.warwick-castle.com
Admission charge

Gardens

THE MASTER'S GARDEN
Lord Leycester Hospital
Tel. 01926 491422
www.lordleycester.co.uk
Small admission charge

PAGEANT GARDENS
Small public gardens
Castle Street
Admission Free

THE MILL GARDEN
Mill Street
Tel. 01926 492877
Small admission charge

THE FRIENDS MEETING HOUSE
GARDENS
39 High Street
Tel. 01926 497732
Admission Free

COLLEGE GARDENS
The Butts – or entry from St Mary's churchyard
Admission Free

ST JOHN'S HOUSE GARDEN
Tel. 01926 412132 or 412021
www.warwickshire.gov.uk
Admission free

HILL CLOSE GARDENS
Bread and Meat Close (off Friars Street)
Tel. 01926 493339
www.hillclosegardens.com
Admission charge

ST NICHOLAS PARK
Banbury Road
Tel. 01926 410410
Leisure Centre 01926 450000

WARWICK COMMON
Within the racecourse circuit
Access from Friar Street

Places to Stay in Historic Warwick

LORD LEYCESTER HOTEL
19 Jury Street
Warwick CV34 4EJ
Tel. 01926 491481
www.lord-leycester.co.uk

WARWICK ARMS HOTEL
High Street
Warwick
CV34 4AT
Tel. 01926 492759
www.warwickarmshotel.com

THE LAZY COW HOTEL
10 Theatre Street
Tel. 0845 120 0666
www.thelazycowwarwick.co.uk